OVERLOOK

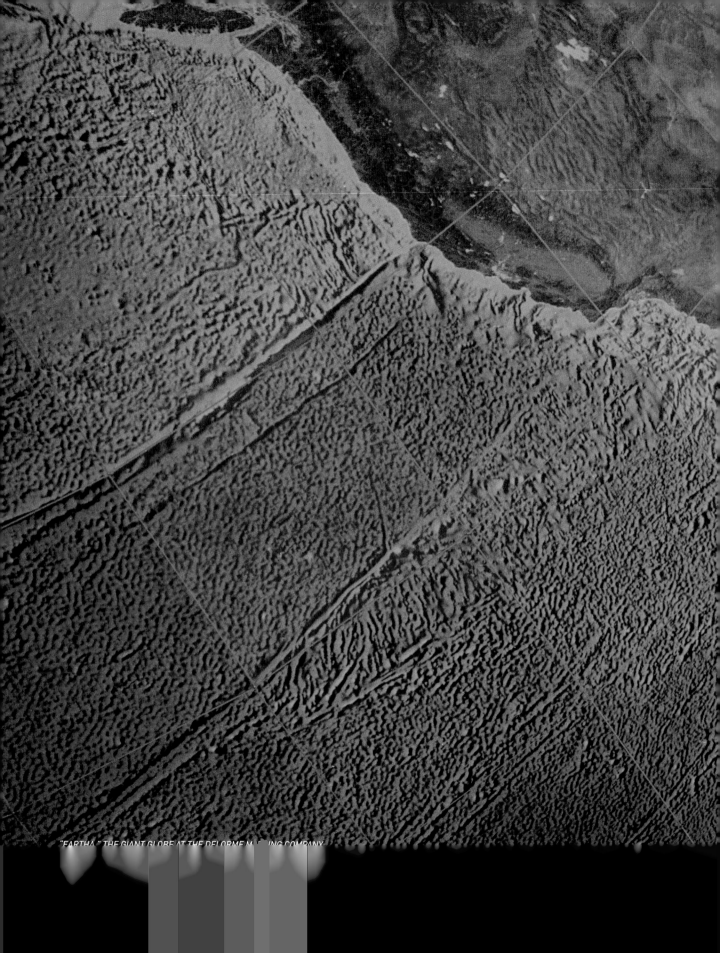

EACH OF US STANDS AT THE CENTER OF OUR UNIVERSE AND GAZES OUT AT THE WORLD.

VISITORS AT THE NIAGARA FALLS OVERLOOK

OUR VIEW IS OFTEN FOCUSED AND FRAMED
BY THE INSTITUTIONS THAT GUIDE SOCIETY.

INTERPRETIVE ISLAND, WASHINGTON STATE

ALTHOUGH THERE ARE MANY WAYS OF LOOKING
AT A SINGLE PLACE,

COLUMBIA RIVER OVERLOOK, WASHINGTON STATE

Wheatfield
Colu

Samuel Hill
Memorial Bridge

Biggs, OR.

Rufus, OR.

John Day Dam

Maryhill, WA.

Stonehenge, 3 miles

the S
of Seattle, W

WE FIND A WIDER VIEW FROM AN OVERLOOK.

Deschutes River Canyon

Miller Island

Mt. Hood,
elevation 11,235 ft.

Horsethief Lake, 14 miles

Edited by
MATTHEW COOLIDGE
and SARAH SIMONS

OVERLOOK:
Exploring the Internal Fringes of America
with the Center for Land Use Interpretation

METROPOLIS BOOKS

Available through D.A.P./
Distributed Art Publishers, Inc.,
New York

METROPOLIS BOOKS
is a joint publishing program of:

D.A.P. / Distributed Art Publishers, Inc.
155 Sixth Avenue, 2nd floor
New York NY 10013
tel 212 627 1999
fax 212 627 9484
www.artbook.com

and

Metropolis Magazine
61 West 23rd Street, 4th floor
New York NY 10010
tel 212 627 9977
fax 212 627 9988
www.metropolismag.com

METROPOLIS
BOOKS

Editor: Diana Murphy
Production editors: Jane Brown and Janet Parker
Designers: Lorraine Wild and Stuart Smith, Green Dragon Office, Los Angeles

Separations and printing: Asia Pacific Offset, Inc., China

Set in FF Bau, FF DIN and **Interstate** and printed on NPI matt art

Library of Congress Cataloging-in-Publication Data

Overlook : exploring the internal fringes of America with the Center for Land Use Interpretation / edited by Matthew Coolidge and Sarah Simons.
p. cm.
ISBN 1-933045-33-7
1. United States—Geography—Miscellanea. 2. United States—Description and travel—Miscellanea. 3. Land use—United States—Miscellanea. 4. Landscape—United States—Miscellanea. 5. Landscape architecture—United States—Miscellanea. 6. Public spaces—United States—Miscellanea. 7. Public lands—United States—Miscellanea. 8. Human geography—United States—Miscellanea. 9. Human ecology—United States—Miscellanea. 10. United States—History, Local—Miscellanea. I. Coolidge, Matthew. II. Simons, Sarah, 1959– III. Center for Land Use Interpretation.
E161.3.O84 2006
917.3'02—dc22

2006010263

Page 1: Pilot Peak overlook, Nevada

Pages 10–11: View of the exhibit *Territory in Photo-Color: The Postcards of Merle Porter* at CLUI: Los Angeles, 1999

CONTENTS

PREFACE

This book shares some completed and ongoing Center for Land Use Interpretation projects, selected to represent an interpretive arc around the country. Since the United States is just too big to get your mind around the whole thing, you have to look at it in pieces. One way of doing that is to take a basic, representative state like Ohio, and see what's there. That is chapter one. Another way is to shrink the landscape down to a manageable size. "Terrestrial Miniaturizations" (chapter two) shows that nobody has done this better and bigger than the Army Corps of Engineers, whose three large models of portions of America are overlooked engineering wonders. One can also peer beneath the surface, go underground, and find a version of the country that has evolved in transformed natural caverns (chapter three) or that has been flooded and lurks beneath some of the thousands of artificial lakes and reservoirs across the land (chapter four). People who work in the emergency professions, like police and fire crews, have created hybrid and disaster versions of regular landscapes to practice on. These "mock towns" and training sites are distillations of the places Americans live (chapter five). There are also regions that, due to qualities of their geography, have developed unique characteristics that help us to understand the bigger picture of this country. Chapter six looks at one of these regions, what we call Federaland, which is "away" for all of us who don't live there, and home for those of us who do.

The Editors

MATTHEW COOLIDGE

INTRODUCTION

FOR MANY READERS, this book might serve as an introduction to the Center for Land Use Interpretation. But it's my hope that, after reading it, you forget about us – the Center. You can even forget the information about the sites we describe in this volume. (It remains in print and on the Internet, should you need to retrieve it). In fact, you can even forget the very point that is being made right now. What matters is that after reading this book, or after encountering any of our programming elsewhere, you come away with a widened sense of awareness of the physical world that surrounds you.

The work of the Center is about humans and the land they inhabit and transform. It is about how we, individually and collectively, interact with each other and with our surroundings. Think of a "typical" American life as moving between such land-use sites as hospitals, houses, schools, parks, roads, parking lots, churches, factories, office buildings, job sites, shopping centers, restaurants, and cemeteries. Such a life might also directly or indirectly be supported by places like landfills, utility corridors, airports, shipping terminals, power plants, subway tunnels, oil fields, bombing ranges, and golf courses. And so on.

The marks we leave on the ground can be intentional, incidental, or accidental. They can be vast in scale, like a housing development, or hardly noticeable, like pipe casing or a switchbox. All of this can be read, like a text, a text that tells stories about our culture and society. Learning how to read this text, learning the vocabulary of the language of land use and teaching it to others, is one way of describing what the Center does. The shared space of the earth is physically and metaphorically what unites us, and until we colonize space, what we have here on this planet is all we have to work with. So it makes sense to investigate the human experience from the ground up.

Surely, there are others at work in this arena. Archeologists excavate the past from the ground, historians assimilate moments into patterns, and cultural theorists apply the structures of history to the present. Elsewhere on the ground, geologists study the subsurface, geomorphologists scrutinize the surface, and geographers examine the systems of human and nonhuman activities. All of their readings help us to understand how we got to this point, and how things look from their point of view. But there are other parts of the spectrum of perception left unexplored by scholars, scientists, and other specialists – dimensions that are only hinted at in the great museums of the land.

The answers to much of what remains unclear to us are exposed for all to see, though often hidden, as it were, in plain sight. They can often be found in the overlooked quotidian elements that surround us, too banal-seeming to have value in any larger equation. Yet these are the building blocks of existence. Often, due to the fashion of the day, some things are perceived as being ugly, so we turn away from them; as a result they remain a mystery for us to come back to another time. Even more often, whole avenues of experience lie unexplored because no one has yet wandered down these roads with the attentiveness they deserve.

The Center's role is partly to explore these corridors and vistas and to trip over the protruding artifacts of the present on the way to explaining the extraordinary conditions we all find ourselves in all the time. As we stumble over the obvious, we ask ourselves, "What is that thing anyway, and how did it get there?" The results are compiled, sorted, processed, and stored in our Land Use Database.

The database is the foundation of the organization, an informational bedrock. It is from this collection that we draw in order to produce our programming. It is also a resource for others, primarily for research and educational purposes. We make a certain amount of it available on our website, a geographically and thematically searchable collection of more than a thousand selected locations across the United States.

Raw material comes to the database through research on specific projects and from a network of informal sources, mostly individuals who send it in as they come across it. It takes the form of notes scribbled while driving, articles clipped from trade journals, pamphlets, photographs, annotated maps, addresses on the web, and published documents describing places. However it comes to the Center, and whatever form it takes, this material is sorted and stored in electronic and physical files – or discarded.

THE CENTER FOR LAND USE INTERPRETATION MAINTAINS A DATABASE
OF INFORMATION ON UNUSUAL AND EXEMPLARY SITES THROUGHOUT THE
UNITED STATES. THIS FREE, PUBLIC RESOURCE IS DESIGNED TO EDUCATE
AND INFORM THE PUBLIC ABOUT THE FUNCTION AND FORM OF THE
NATIONAL LANDSCAPE, A TERRESTRIAL SYSTEM THAT HAS BEEN ALTERED
TO ACCOMMODATE THE COMPLEX DEMANDS OF OUR SOCIETY.

The database is not a collection of everything, but rather a selection from everything. It is an inventory of examples. Its utility would be limited if it were unfiltered and exhaustive — too much information can be as obfuscating as too little. The Center applies the "unusual and exemplary" criteria in order to limit the information that is preserved. These criteria, while institutionally subjective, guide an informed process that has been refined over the life of the organization, drawing from the knowledge, experience, and education of the people at the Center.

The Center regards a site as "unusual" if it stands out as unique, extraordinary, singular, rare, or exceptional. An example might be a piece of land art or a plutonium processing facility. A site is considered "exemplary" if it serves well to represent a more common type of land use, if it is especially articulate, descriptive, coherent, or concise. Or if it represents an apogee of its type: perhaps it's the first, the largest, the smallest, or has some other superlative quality. In this case, it is selected to exemplify that form of land use.

Together these criteria reduce the landscape into expressive parts. The resulting collection is inclusive, but it's not a complete inventory, and rather than imply that everything has been discovered, it suggests that there is more to be discovered than we might have ever imagined.

PHOTOGRAPHER STEVE ROWELL
IN THE FIELD

ERIK KNUTZEN LEADING A TOUR AT A DEBRIS DAM

WHILE A SITE NEEDN'T BE ACCESSIBLE, OPEN TO THE PUBLIC, OR EVEN VISITABLE, ALL DATABASE ENTRIES NEED TO BE DISTINCT PHYSICAL PLACES. THEY CAN BE LARGE OR SMALL IN SIZE, BUT THEY HAVE TO BE LOCATABLE. IN THE DATABASE, THEY ARE GEOGRAPHICALLY REFERENCED BY A STREET ADDRESS OR BY COORDINATES OF LONGITUDE AND LATITUDE.

Once a site has been selected for inclusion in the database, a member of the Center's staff writes a brief synopsis about it. This text encapsulates the form and function of the site, conveying its character, its qualities, and, implicitly, why it was singled out. This paragraph or so is written with precision, and in simple language, for a general audience.

Since humans are visual creatures, images constitute a critical part of the database. The Center's photographic archive describes the sites in the database in ways that text cannot. These thousands of images have all been taken by the Center's representatives and volunteers over the years since the founding of the organization. While every site in the database does not have an image, it should, and is expected to over time. Many of the images are taken by professional artists and photographers, but nearly all are donated to the Center for unrestricted use and without any attribution. The function of this anonymity is to let the image, as much as it can, stand for itself, as a document. It is not meant to be a record of an individual photographer's point of view, but an institutionalized record of the appearance of a place.

By avoiding the use of existing photographs, which might be readily available from the representatives of the site or from other agencies or constituencies, the Center's photographic archive offers an independent view and a primary level of site verification. Images are generally taken during site visits, essential encounters that the Center and its agents conduct as often as possible.

These site visits are made when resources permit or when called for as part of a specific thematic or regional program. Site visits are sometimes coordinated through the owners or managers of the site. When this is not possible, images are generally taken from public property at or adjacent to the site. In some cases, aerial photographs are the most descriptive, and photographers associated with the Center often turn to this platform.

In addition to procuring images, researchers take notes and write descriptions of the places they visit, following the Center's Site Characterization Report guidelines. Independent field researchers – that is, individuals who voluntarily submit material to the Center – do so using forms like this one to the right:

FIELD RESEARCHER SITE-CHARACTERIZATION FORM

SITE NAME

What do they (the owners/managers of the site) call it? Or what do others in the area call it? Or, if both of these are unknown, what do you call it? (usually the title describes the function of the site, such as in "Underwater Nuclear Warfare Center," or "The Barbed Wire Museum")

_____

_____

WHAT IS IT?

Describe the function of the site or the activity that is pursued there, as well as any information that might be important to visitors, such as accessibility, toxic hazards, admission charge, etc. _____

_____

WHERE IS IT?

Locate in relation to nearest town and roadway (for example: "ten miles southeast of Roswell off highway 380"). Submit GPS coordinates if possible.

_____

_____

IS THERE A STREET ADDRESS OR A MAILING ADDRESS?

STREET ADDRESS: _____

CITY: _____ STATE: _____

ZIP: _____ PHONE: _____

LIST WEBSITES HERE

Send additional information including maps, articles, images, etc.

_____   _____   _____

_____   _____   _____

YOUR NAME: _____

E-MAIL ADDRESS: _____

STREET ADDRESS: _____

CITY: _____ STATE: _____

ZIP: _____ PHONE: _____

LAND-USE CLASSIFICATION LIST

CHECK ANY KEYWORDS THAT APPLY

The purpose of keywords is to allow searches of the database to generate interesting and useful groupings. Although keyword searches of the database do scan the text associated with the site, keywords are weighted differently.

☐ Abandoned
☐ Accident Site
☐ Agriculture/Horticulture
☐ Airport
☐ Alternative Technology
☐ Analog Environment
☐ Aqueduct
☐ Architectural/Sculptural Landmark
☐ Art
☐ Attraction
☐ Automotive
☐ Aviation
☐ Aviation/Aerospace Museum
☐ Beacon
☐ Bicycle
☐ Bombing
☐ Bottled Water Source
☐ Boundary
☐ Canal
☐ Cement Plant
☐ Cemetery
☐ Chemical Plant
☐ Chemical Waste Site
☐ Command Center
☐ Communications
☐ Computer Technology Facility
☐ Contaminated
☐ Control Center
☐ Correctional Facility
☐ Dam
☐ Defense
☐ Disposal Site
☐ Distribution Center
☐ DOE (Department of Energy)
☐ Dry Lake
☐ Dump/Landfill
☐ Electrical Distribution
☐ Emergency Response
☐ Environmental
☐ Expo
☐ Federal
☐ Festival
☐ Film/TV Location
☐ Finance
☐ Flood Control
☐ Food
☐ Forestry
☐ Former Industrial Site
☐ Formerly Used Defense Site
☐ Ghost Town

☐ Gravel Pit
☐ Groundwater/Aquifer
☐ Headquarters
☐ Housing
☐ ICBM Silo
☐ Incinerator
☐ Industrial Site
☐ Intelligence
☐ Intentional Community
☐ International Border Site
☐ Land Art
☐ Manufacturing/Processing Facility
☐ Marine
☐ Medical/Health Care Facility
☐ Metals Manufacturing
☐ Military
☐ Military Base
☐ Military Museum
☐ Milling
☐ Miniature
☐ Mining
☐ Monument
☐ Munitions Plant/Ordnance Depot
☐ Museum
☐ Native American Site
☐ Natural Feature
☐ Nuclear Power Plant
☐ Nuclear/Radioactive
☐ Nuclear Weapons Base
☐ Observatory
☐ Office
☐ OHV (Off-Highway Vehicle) Recreation Area
☐ Open Pit
☐ Park
☐ Parking Lot
☐ Pedestrian
☐ Petrochemical Extraction
☐ Physics
☐ Pier/Jetty/Shoreline Structure
☐ Pipeline
☐ Police
☐ Pond/Lake
☐ Port
☐ Power Plant/Electrical Generation
☐ Processing
☐ Public Safety Training Facility
☐ Pumping Station
☐ Quarry
☐ R&D (Research and Development)

☐ Race Track
☐ Radar
☐ Railway
☐ Railway Bridge
☐ Railway Tunnel
☐ Rail Yard
☐ Range
☐ Recreation Site
☐ Reenactment Site
☐ Reservoir
☐ River
☐ Road
☐ Road Bridge
☐ Roadway Tunnel
☐ Ruin
☐ Sculpture
☐ Sculpture Park
☐ Shelter
☐ Shipyard
☐ Shooting Range
☐ Shopping Center
☐ Space
☐ Sports Facility
☐ Spring
☐ Storage
☐ Store
☐ Submarine
☐ Submerged
☐ Tailings
☐ Telecommunications
☐ Testing
☐ Textiles
☐ Theme and Amusement
☐ Toll Booth
☐ Tourist Cave
☐ Town/Community
☐ Training
☐ Transportation Site
☐ Treatment Plant
☐ Tunnel
☐ UFO Site
☐ Underground
☐ Utopia
☐ Visitors' Center
☐ Waste
☐ Waste Transfer Site
☐ Water Site
☐ Water Treatment

The Center's Land Use Database is a record of America in this time as well as a dynamic, self-serve portrait of the nation. It is a resource for referencing singular or exceptional phenomena, and for making connections between things, discovering linkages from local sites to larger, nationwide systems. The database is a tool that enables its users to explore remotely, to search obliquely, and to make creative collisions and juxtapositions that render new meanings and explanations of America – and of the many ways of looking at it.

When the Center initiates a public exhibit, a publication, or a tour program, it is generally of a regional or thematic nature, or a combination of the two. Thematic programs look at a particular aspect of the built landscape, a phenomenon that may occur in several or numerous instances across the country. In a regional program, the area of study is geographically limited in some way, for example by a state, county, or municipal boundary. In a combination, a thematic project is conducted within a defined region.

One of the functions of a regional program is to characterize the region by describing its built landscape, and in this way to offer a portrait of its economy, its culture, and its identity. The elements of this landscape, from the Center's perspective, are the Land Use Database sites within it. Often it is necessary to conduct additional research and photography of the region before arriving at a coherent and up-to-date characterization. This work is supported by volunteer researchers or by a research grant from a host institution, a government agency, or a foundation. Once the additional field research and photography are completed, the new information is entered in the database, and remains there to support additional regional or thematic projects in the future.

When engaging in a regional project, the Center poses an initial set of questions to establish the degree to which field research is necessary and then begins the process of putting together the project. These questions might include: Where do people work (what are the major employers and industries in the region)? Where does their food come from? Where does their water come from? Where does their waste (liquid and solid) go? Where does their energy come from? Where and how do they live (housing developments, apartments, urban/rural)? How do they get around (roads, trains, public transportation)? Once these questions are addressed by consulting the database and by conducting library and Internet research, a program of field research can begin. It is often in this phase that many of the most interesting elements of the place emerge; things are discovered just by looking attentively at the region and reading the landscape itself for clues.

If the project is thematic in nature, then research begins with the database, as sites are examined for their relevance to the theme or subject of the project. Keywords associated with each site — such as "underground," "ruin," or "housing" — facilitate such cross-index searches. Additional library, Internet, and field research may also be required, depending on the specificity of the theme. As with regional projects, information and imagery obtained for thematic projects help to enhance the database for future uses.

The Center presents exhibits at its own facilities as well as at other public venues, such as museums and university galleries. The exhibits are also published on the Web. They employ a variety of documentary media to describe the places they depict, such as text, photography, aerial and satellite images, maps, video, and even live feeds and live sound. In some cases, another form of representation is also arranged, one that permits a direct experience with the places depicted: the guided tour. Usually conducted on a video-equipped luxury bus, these tours are choreographed excursions into the field, sometimes lasting two days. Open to the public, the tours take participants through a carefully researched route, timed with stops and meetings with local experts at the sites. An informed live narration takes place throughout, and a program of video on overhead monitors is also timed to give background, context, or foreshadowing of the places the tour is traveling to, by, or through.

THE CENTER'S GUIDED BUS TOURS HAVE BEEN DESCRIBED
AS A "MULTIMEDIA PHENOMENOLOGICAL ODYSSEY" AND
A "SPATIOTEMPORAL, NONFICTIONAL THEATER PRODUCTION,
BROUGHT OUT TO THE LANDSCAPE."

A PARTICIPANT IN THE CENTER'S WENDOVER RESIDENCE PROGRAM WORKS ON A WIND-POWERED, ROVING SCULPTURE OUTSIDE THE ENOLA GAY HANGAR. THE PROGRAM FOSTERS CREATIVE INTERPRETATIONS OF THE REGION AROUND WENDOVER, UTAH.

THE DESERT RESEARCH STATION NEAR BARSTOW, CALIFORNIA,
IS ONE OF A GROWING NETWORK OF REGIONAL RESEARCH,
PRODUCTION, AND PRESENTATION VENUES OPERATED BY THE CENTER.

THE CENTER CONDUCTS FIELD TRIPS FOR CLASSES, USUALLY
AT THE GRADUATE LEVEL. THESE TRIPS OFTEN EXAMINE SITES
OF PARTICULAR INTEREST AND SIGNIFICANCE IN REGIONS AROUND
THE CENTER'S FIELD FACILITIES.

THE CENTER PRESENTS EXHIBITS AT ITS OWN FACILITIES, AT MUSE-
UMS, AND AT OTHER NONCOMMERCIAL VENUES. THE CENTER'S
OFFICE AND DISPLAY LOCATION IN LOS ANGELES IS OPEN TO THE
PUBLIC AND FEATURES PERMANENT AND ROTATING EXHIBITS, A
BOOKSHOP, AND A LIBRARY.

If we think of the contemporary landscape as a kind of museum, a repository containing some of the material culture of our time, the importance of direct contact with these artifacts of the ground cannot be overstated. We all remember things and places a lot better when we see and touch them ourselves. Afterward, we imagine them as real, rather than imagined. Beyond the tours, another way that the Center helps people to experience the landscape directly is by providing interpretive sites throughout the landscape itself. These interpretive sites are both destinations — places to go to — and points of departure, for exploring the transformed landscapes of the nation. These sites range in form from interpretive plaques, standing alone all by themselves, to information centers and exhibit sites that are open to the public.

At the moment, and for the foreseeable future, the Center limits its investigations to the United States. This is partially due to practical considerations: it's a big world, and the Center has a relatively small staff. But the principal reason is that the United States is a fascinating, complex, misunderstood, and important place. It has emerged quickly from a self-sustaining, isolated world in itself to the internationally engaged global power of today. In this rapid transformation, much has been left unconsidered, cast aside, or just passed by.

Repeated travel over the same road increases our familiarity with it, and we think we come to know it better and better. But patterns and ways of seeing can form, regulating our perceptive apparatus in ways that limit our ability to sense the rest of the spectrum. The more we think we know something, more of it becomes lost to us. Experiential habits become common corridors of perception that merge into the superhighways of convention. To avert whatever crisis might be forming in the present and awaiting us in the future, the world needs to maintain its interpretive diversity, along with its biological and cultural diversity. The tool kit needs to be fully stocked.

MULTIPLE INTERPRETIVE LAYERS AT THE PROJECT GNOME SITE,
NEAR CARLSBAD, NEW MEXICO

THE PERCEPTION OF A PLACE IS AFFECTED BY EACH
OF THE MEDIATING AGENTS IT PASSES THROUGH, FROM
THE INERT MATERIAL OF THE GROUND TO THE FINAL
FRAME OF THE BEHOLDER.

IMAGE FROM THE EXHIBIT LOOP FEEDBACK LOOP: THE BIG PICTURE OF TRAFFIC CONTROL IN LOS ANGELES, *2004*

THE CENTER FOR LAND USE INTERPRETATION is one of the most intelligently provocative organizations that I have ever had the good fortune to encounter. What exactly it is up to is another matter, but before I wade into the muddy waters of speculation regarding the Center's possible functions — which are not at all obvious — a few facts are in order. The Center is a nonprofit educational organization that examines how we use, envision, and think about different kinds of landscapes in the United States. A few individuals from different backgrounds who nonetheless had come to think and work in similar ways founded the Center in 1994 in Oakland, California. Operating out of a rickety office along that city's industrial waterfront, they began presenting exhibits that examined areas where the man-made, the cultural, and the natural seemed to merge. They also conducted tours focusing on little-observed features of the surrounding urban area, and installed interpretive plaques commemorating unusual types of land use (such as one marking a site in New

RALPH RUGOFF

CIRCLING THE CENTER

Mexico where in 1957 a hydrogen bomb hit the ground after having been accidentally dropped from an airplane).

Audiences for these initial programs were small, but that was of little consequence. What mattered was that the Center was inventing, piece by piece, a new type of institution: a grassroots clearinghouse that presented documentation of the curious, astonishing, and sometimes alarming transformations of the contemporary American landscape. Looking at material that was off the radar of both the mass media and mainstream academia, the Center's programs addressed not only the way that land is used, but also how it is perceived. To a certain extent, even, it could be said that its real subject is how we look at, and conceptualize, the world around us (but more on that later).

I first picked up on the Center in 1996 after it had relocated to Los Angeles, opening a small office next to another unique organization, the Museum of Jurassic Technology. The Center's exhibits in its new home continued to look at aspects of how the country's lands are used and perceived, examining an eclectic array of sites ranging from field-test facilities for high-impact technologies to sites of "geo-transformative" activity undertaken by government agencies. Among other memorable exhibits from those days were a display of aerial photographs of open-pit mines, shot as a hobby by a retired mining engineer, that were disconcertingly beautiful, and a screening program featuring films of nuclear testing programs of the world's declared nuclear powers (which was a study of different cultural approaches to propaganda as much as it was about perspectives on land use).

Over the years, the Center's exhibits and publications have been remarkably astute, noteworthy not only for illuminating our understand-

IMAGE FROM THE EXHIBIT EAST CENTRAL INTERCEPTOR SEWER: A VIEW INTO THE PIPE, *2004*

ing of mundane as well as extraordinary landscapes, but also for their evenhanded and lucid exposition. Even when describing odd, disturbing, or even potentially humorous phenomena, the tenor of these presentations is never dramatic or self-conscious. Texts tend to be straightforward and factually oriented, while the Center's photographs typically resemble the seemingly authorless images compiled in government and industrial archives (though, for the most part, these photographs are produced by the Center's extended family of volunteers). In their tone, at least, these programs conjure the work of a benevolent social science

RUGOFF

agency or think tank, or perhaps a forward-looking research division of the U.S. Army Corps of Engineers. (The Center's name likewise suggests some such bureaucratic organization). And as it has grown over the past decade, this organization has in many very real ways come to resemble a public research institute, developing an impressive array of databases, libraries, and archives as well as far-flung "research training stations" and myriad outreach programs.

Yet unlike its institutional counterparts, the Center has remained curiously unmoored from any recognizable policy platform. Its programs – as far as I can discern – reveal no overt or even implicit political or social agenda. Indeed, whether documenting nuclear proving grounds or the architecture of show caves (subterranean caverns that have been decorated and turned into tourist attractions), its exhibitions and publications are always disarmingly – at times, almost unnervingly – free of any editorial viewpoint. They are equally detached from the positions of environmental politics as from those of the military or commercial industry.

But if this organization is not trying to sell us an ideological bag of goods, what purpose(s) could possibly be motivating its public exploration of how land is used and apportioned in the United States? It is not only the more cynical among us who may regard the Center's ostensible neutrality, its flagrant nonpartisanship, as slightly suspicious as well as provocative. Its nonjudgmental attitude goes against the grain of our expectations, especially when it is applied to contentious subjects like nuclear weapons testing or strip-mining, which we are accustomed to considering within an explicitly political or moral framework.

This conspicuous absence of editorial slant is paralleled by the expansive – almost indiscriminate – selection criteria used by the Center in choosing subjects for its exhibitions and publications. Besides reportage on such topics as shipping channels, defense installations, and aspects of urban infrastructure, the Center's purview embraces less straightforward phenomena: underwater towns created by dam-produced floods; fictionalized spaces ranging from movie set locations to civilian emergency training sites where life-size props simulate toxic fuel spills and collapsing buildings; and the alternative universe of the Nellis Range, a five-thousand-square-mile area of military-controlled terrain in Nevada, which since 1940 has been a virtual nation unto itself, a kind of time capsule cut off from the rest of American society. Significantly, the Center treats all these diverse subjects in an identical manner, assigning no more weight to an exhibit on anti-terrorist barricades than to one looking at period travel postcards. Within the broadly defined field of "land use interpretation," they are all comparably noteworthy.

In this way the Center's programs deliberately bypass the familiar categories and classifications that we rely on in making sense of the world. A very curious effect results from this benignly subversive approach: we may end up looking at one place or activity through a lens we normally reserve for evaluating another. By treating a nuclear test site in the same manner as an outdoor sculpture, for instance, the Center's exhibits gently prompt us to reconsider the sculpture as possible waste while appreciating the aesthetic value of the radioactive hole (think of it as a type of vast earthwork). In engineering this subtle shift, the Center introduces us to a landscape of uncertainty where our ready-made convictions and judgments lose their traction. But it undermines our assumptions in a very generous manner, encouraging us to look at things from more than one perspective and alerting us to other ways of understanding that can renew our interest in the larger landscape.

From another point of view, of course, it can be argued that the Center's apparent lack of editorial bias is itself a kind of editorial stance – though one directed not against any particular issue so much as the fallibility of our knowledge in general. Indeed, a tonic trace of skepticism runs just beneath the surface of many of the Center's activities, including its archival projects that involve ordering mountains of information

IMAGE FROM THE EXHIBIT PROXIMITY ISSUE: THE BARRICADES OF THE FEDERAL DISTRICT, *2002*

RUGOFF

so they can be productively mined. Yet even while it divides this material into categories and subcategories, indexing it with keywords and cross-references, the Center seems to subtly acknowledge that its own ordering system is inevitably flawed — that to arbitrarily classify things and place them in conceptual cubbyholes involves cutting them off from the continuum of existence.

In contrast to our culture of experts — the pundits, academics, and government analysts who regularly appear in the media to tell us what to think — the Center is a haven of amateur agnostics. Its members are

IMAGE FROM THE EXHIBIT THE VORs OF TEXAS, *1998*

specialists who specialize in nonspecialization. Their approach is not so much multidisciplinary as nondisciplinary: it traces out an underlying logic that connects disparate fields and perspectives, linking them to the common ground of land use and its interpretation. And on one level, at least, it speaks to a desire to transcend the increasingly differentiated, specialized, and disconnected worlds of science, commerce, culture, and politics.

To a certain extent, I think of the Center as a type of informational test site or lab where different models of presenting data are tried out and developed. In the process, its far-ranging programs have also charted an alternative map of the United States. Filling in blank spots in our collective perceptual field, they call attention to neglected, overlooked, and often highly telling aspects of the American landscape. And once exposed to this information, our everyday picture of the world around us—and our sense of our role in it — can never be the same again. Yet the specifics of how our perspective may change is something that each visitor works out

IMAGE FROM THE EXHIBIT NELLIS RANGE COMPLEX: LANDSCAPE OF CONJECTURE, *1999*

on his or her own. The Center is not interested in lobbying us for a particular point of view or trying to mold our opinions. It simply suggests that things might be different than we had previously thought.

In other words, the Center never pretends to have all the answers. Instead, its programs suggest that answers often come in the form of questions, and as the result of finding the ground beneath the middle of an apparent conflict. That conflict may be one of values. Many of the Center's projects emphasize the contradictory qualities of a given subject: a suburban landscape that is at once banal and melodramatic, an industrial harbor that is simultaneously unsightly and sublime. If the Center has a function — and I am not at all sure it does, at least not in any conventional sense — it might have something to do with recognizing and celebrating this kind of paradoxical perspective, and with disseminating the idea that truth exists only in conditions of contradiction.

Yet I suspect that the Center, however indirectly, also functions as an agent of intelligent change, possibly even revolutionary change. Its politics are oblique, of course, and it may be that they are most conspicuous in terms of the Center's decentralized organizational model. A largely volunteer outfit with contributors from across the country, independently researching and investigating and producing new materials about land use and its interpretation, the Center has continued to develop in unpredictable directions (I long ago lost track of how many desert research outposts, interpretative stations, and regional offices it has opened around the country). Distributing the fruits of this open-source research in myriad forms (including its excellent website and printed newsletter, *The Lay of the Land*), the Center eschews any central voice of authority. It presents no master narrative that demands an exclusive path of action. Its politics, if they can be described in such terms, are indirect and elusive. They evade conventional forms by refusing to embrace recognizable "positions" — positions that easily become reified postures that can be targeted and dismissed. Embracing a post-protest ethic that moves beyond simple binary oppositions, the Center sets out to reframe the nature of debate itself. Its work confronts contradiction and gray areas, prompting us to question the points of balance in our existing notions about land use and to grapple with the daunting complexities and scenarios of contemporary landscapes. It presents opportunities for opening up new avenues of knowledge rather than reinforcing ready-made conclusions. Needless to say, the question of land use is an area of increasing concern, and I imagine that the future impact of this organization's work will grow exponentially in the years ahead. Of course, what we do with the awareness it provokes is up to each of us in the end, but on its own the Center is already evolving tools that can transform the way we think — not only about politics, but about the very ground beneath us all.

FOR EXAMPLE, LET'S LOOK AT OHIO. IT OFFERS A GOOD CROSS-SECTION OF AMERICAN DEMOGRAPHICS, AS SO MANY MARKET RESEARCHERS HAVE LONG KNOWN. IT'S URBAN, IT'S RURAL; IT'S GOT BIG CITIES, SMALL TOWNS; IT'S GOT AGRICULTURE, MINING, SUBURBAN SPRAWL, AND HEAVY INDUSTRY. IT'S WHITE, BLACK, BROWN, AND YELLOW; COSMOPOLITAN IN SOME PLACES, LESS SO IN OTHERS. IT'S IN THE MIDDLE OF THE EASTERN HALF OF THE COUNTRY, NOT QUITE

Northeast and just barely Midwest, with several counties even lying within Appalachia. It's neither here nor there; it's everywhere. Very arguably, it is the most "all-American" state, and thus a good place to get an overview of the country.

Although Ohio may not literally be round on its edges, we know at least how high it is in the middle (1,549 feet). It is a major state for transportation industries (cars and planes), consumer goods, and energy production. After the "big generals" (General Motors and General Electric), the next largest employers in the state are Kroger (groceries) and Wal-Mart, which provide workers with much of their food, clothing, and consumer goods. Ohio also boasts some places that are unique and vital to national programs, including two NASA test and development sites and several nuclear plants dedicated to enriching and processing radioactive materials. The state's official, optimistic motto is "With God, all things are possible." Who could argue with that?

**1
ROUND ON THE EDGES:
LET'S LOOK AT OHIO**

produce Chevy Cavaliers and Pontiac Sunfires at a rate of more than sixty-five cars every hour, 325,000 per year. GM's other large Ohio plant, in Moraine, makes sport utility vehicles like Blazers and Jimmys. Daimler-Chrysler makes Jeeps in Toledo, and Ford makes vans in Lorain and Avon Lake. Two Honda plants near Marysville produce more than 650,000 Accords, Accuras, and Civics a year.

GENERAL MOTORS, often ranked as the largest corporation in the world (along with Wal-Mart), is the largest corporate employer in Ohio, with more than twenty thousand employees. Ohio is the second-largest car manufacturing state in the country. The GM plant in Lordstown, outside Youngsville in the eastern part of the state, is one of five major automobile assembly plants in Ohio owned by the Big Three and sits adjacent to a metals fabrication plant. Its five thousand workers

GENERAL MOTORS LORDSTOWN PLANT

PROCTER AND GAMBLE IVORYDALE

IVORYDALE IS a factory complex of 120 buildings on 243 acres that dates back to 1885, when Procter and Gamble's operations expanded from its original location in downtown Cincinnati. Still inside the city limits, it takes its name from Ivory soap, one of P&G's earliest and most successful products. Other products manufactured at the Ivorydale complex, which employs thirteen hundred workers, include Crisco shortening, Tide laundry soap, and Crest toothpaste. The Cincinnati-based consumer product company is one of the rare manufacturers that can claim, accurately, to distribute its brands to the majority of the earth's six billion people.

THE MEAD Paper Company has operated a paper mill in Chillicothe since 1890,
and for a brief period the company had
its headquarters here. The Chillicothe
facility is the largest of three Mead mills in
the United States, employing more than
two thousand people and producing half
a million tons of paper annually. Mead,
a global paper company now based in Dayton, does four billion dollars in annual
sales. It recently doubled in size by merging
with another paper company, Westvaco,
and is now owned by the MeadWestvaco
company, based in Connecticut. It is estimated that as much as 95 percent of Ohio
was forested before farming took hold
in the 1800s. By 1940, forests covered only
12 percent of the state's landscape. Today
that figure is around 30 percent.

**MEAD PAPER
CHILLICOTHE**

MINGO JUNCTION

DESPITE MANY plant closings in recent decades, steel remains a major industry in Ohio. The state ranks among the nation's largest steel producers, employing more than thirty-five thousand people. The plant in Mingo Junction, on the Ohio River, is one of four plants in the state operated by Wheeling-Pittsburgh Steel, the nation's ninth-largest integrated steel company. Like other major regional steel companies, such as LTV, Wheeling-Pittsburgh has been sold and reorganized following bankruptcy. The archetypal town was one of two area steel towns used as a location for the 1978 film *The Deer Hunter*.

BRUSH WELLMAN PLANT

BERYLLIUM IS an element used to make a metal alloy that is lighter than aluminum and harder than steel. It is found in a variety of high-tech and industrial applications, including cell phones, electronics, and dental fixtures. Increased use of beryllium—and the consequent growth of the Brush Wellman company—began with military electronics and nuclear weapons programs following World War II. Based in Cleveland, Brush Wellman is the primary producer and supplier of beryllium products worldwide, and the Elmore plant near Lake Erie is the largest of several that it operates in the United States.

MITCHELLACE PLANT

A PRODUCTIVE RELIC of the American textile era, Mitchellace Inc. produces more than eight million shoelaces every week at this 360,000-square-foot building in Portsmouth, making it still the world's largest manufacturer of shoelaces. This is currently Mitchellace's main production location, but the company plans to open a second plant soon in Honduras.

ROUND ON THE EDGES:

TOWN OF CHESHIRE

AMERICAN ELECTRIC POWER, the nation's largest electrical utility, has bought the two hundred or so lots that make up the small Ohio River town of Cheshire for twenty million dollars, and is expected to tear down the buildings after they are vacated. The company, seeking a larger buffer zone around its James Gavin Power Plant (one of the largest coal-fired plants in the nation), asked all bought-out residents to give up their rights to sue the company for any future health problems, despite residents' claims of burning eyes and throats when the plant occasionally emitted visible clouds of sulfuric acid.

TRANSPORTATION RESEARCH CENTER

THIS 4,500-ACRE operation northwest of Columbus is one of the largest and most diverse independent automotive test sites in the country. A staff of more than six hundred employees runs the site for private and government clients, with facilities that include a 7.5-mile, high-speed, oval test track; an off-road testing area; and a variety of other tracks with different surfaces, from cobblestone to ceramic tile. The center is also a major car-crash test site, with extensive impact research laboratories, crash pads, rollover test areas, and instrumented impact walls.

GENERAL ELECTRIC is the world's leading manufacturer of aircraft engines, many of which are made at its large plant in Evendale, just north of Cincinnati. The company also operates a remote field test station sixty miles outside the city, in the rural, rolling hills near the town of Peebles. The secretive, seven-thousand-acre site has test stands and other support facilities for testing aircraft engines and for various defense projects.

GENERAL ELECTRIC PEEBLES TEST FACILITY

OPERATED BY NASA's Glenn Research Center in Cleveland, Plum Brook is a field-test site spread across sixty-five hundred acres south of Sandusky. Five primary complexes at the site, which was built in the 1960s to support NASA space programs, include some of the world's largest space-simulation test chambers. These indoor facilities can emulate space-like conditions—including a vacuum and temperatures of minus 270 degrees—to test satellite deployment systems and even full-scale, firing rocket engines. There is also a nuclear reactor on premises, which is being decommissioned. A small staff of NASA personnel maintains the site between periodic commercial use by aerospace contractors.

PLUM BROOK FIELD STATION

THIS INDUSTRIAL laboratory and office complex in Columbus is the main lab and headquarters for Battelle, a nonprofit research-and-development institute with more than seventy-five hundred employees at numerous locations. Battelle partners with commercial firms to develop new technologies, including the application of product bar codes and the invention of the photocopier. The lab was established to support the Atomic Energy Commission's work on nuclear weapons. Battelle operates another major facility, the Pacific Northwest National Lab, at the Hanford Nuclear Reservation in Washington, where it has conducted weapons research since the Manhattan Project. Battelle is also the co-manager of the Department of Energy's Oak Ridge National Lab in Tennessee and the Brookhaven National Lab in New York.

BATTELLE INSTITUTE

AKRON BLIMP HANGAR

TIRE PRODUCTION no longer dominates the industrial scene in Akron, the "rubber capital of the world," but Goodyear and B. F. Goodrich still maintain their world headquarters here, with rubber and related polymer research and development continuing in some of the former production facilities. The massive Airdock, one of the most prominent structures remaining from the city's great industrial empire, was built by Goodyear in 1929 for the construction of zeppelins. It is now owned by Lockheed Martin's Naval Electronics and Surveillance Systems division, which continues to build aircraft training systems and blimp-based observation platforms for the Department of Defense.

MINERS MEMORIAL PARK

THE RESTING place for the remaining portion of the "world's largest walking dragline," the bucket for the Big Muskie coal scoop, is the new Miners Memorial Park in Noble County. Big Muskie was the largest of several crane-operated shovels that removed the earth above buried coal seams and recontoured the landscape of southeastern Ohio. (In fact, these draglines moved ten times more earth in Ohio than was moved to create the Panama Canal.) The memorial park sits on the edge of a thirty-thousand-acre former mining area which American Electric Power, the utility that owns it, calls "ReCreation Land." It is also near an active mining area, where high-sulfur coal is still being extracted for power plants along the Ohio River.

MILLFIELD COAL MINE DISASTER SITE

THE APPALACHIAN hills in southeastern Ohio, which continue through much of adjacent West Virginia, contain the largest coal deposits in the eastern United States. They have been mined for nearly two centuries, providing fuel for the industrial revolution in America. Before equipment was invented to remove the massive amounts of soil that covered Ohio's coal deposits, underground mineshafts were the norm, and working conditions were notoriously arduous and dangerous. The worst mining disaster in Ohio occurred here in 1930, when eighty-two people died. Some of the original mining structures remain at the site, overgrown by foliage.

ROUND ON THE EDGES:

PORTSMOUTH GASEOUS DIFFUSION PLANT

ONE OF three major Department of Energy nuclear complex sites in Ohio, the Portsmouth diffusion plant produced enriched uranium for use as fuel in power plants, nuclear submarines, and nuclear weapons. The plant once employed twenty-five hundred people at its thirty-seven-hundred-acre site, which includes some of the largest industrial structures in the world, but most of its operations have shifted to its sister site, the Paducah plant in Kentucky, which is the nation's only other uranium-enrichment plant. The production of high-enriched uranium at the Portsmouth facility ceased in 1991, and low enrichment for commercial power plant fuel ended in 2001. The plant is operated by a private company, the United States Enrichment Corporation, with Lockheed Martin, Bechtel, and others as subcontractors. It is now in cold-standby and clean-up mode, but also conducts programs for the Department of Energy and other contractors. The Portsmouth plant retains the capability to resume uranium enrichment if called upon by the Department of Energy.

OWNED BY the Department of Energy and operated for many years by Monsanto and EG&G, the Mound plant near Dayton produced detonation devices for nuclear weapons and conducted research on nuclear fuels and isotope separation, starting in the 1940s. Now the primary activity at the plant is decontamination of the buildings and grounds in preparation for the expected full conversion to commercial use by 2006. The annual cost of these remediation efforts is about ninety million dollars. The Mound plant is named for a large Indian mound adjacent to the facility. The paved top of the mound provides a good view of the plant.

MOUND PLANT

FERNALD FEED MATERIAL PRODUCTION PLANT

PART OF a nuclear weapons complex developed by the Department of Energy, this plant near Cincinnati originally produced uranium metals for reactors at Hanford, Washington, as well as for some of the department's other weapons facilities. Production ceased in 1989, and the plant is now undergoing cleanup and remediation. The site encompasses nine plants within a 136-acre complex, surrounded by a thousand-acre buffer zone. It employed around one thousand people at its peak, and was operated by Westinghouse. Remediation is being conducted by the Fluor Corporation.

DAVIS-BESSE NUCLEAR POWER PLANT

THE DAVIS-BESSE plant, outside Toledo, is one of two commercial nuclear power plants in Ohio. (The other is the Perry plant, near Cleveland.) Davis-Besse has been shut down for technical problems a few times since going online in 1977. When it was shut down in February 2002 for refueling, operators discovered that boric acid had been dripping onto the reactor head and had eaten away about seventy pounds of steel. The six-inch-deep hole, located in the shell that holds the coolant layer around the reactor core, was three-sixteenths of an inch from going all the way through. Had it ruptured due to the pressure inside, which measures one ton per square inch, it could have produced a catastrophic accident. The First Energy Company of Akron, which owns the plant, repaired the reactor head, and the plant went back online in 2004.

WRIGHT-PATTERSON AIR FORCE BASE

WITH APPROXIMATELY twenty-two thousand employees, this air base in Dayton is the largest single-location employer in Ohio as well as one of the most vital and complex military installations in the country. Many of the advanced weapons systems in the American arsenal have their origins at Wright-Patterson. The base is home to several research-and-development centers, including the Wright Lab, which alone has an annual budget of around one billion dollars. The Air Force Museum, located on the edge of the base, is the largest military aviation museum in the world. Its holdings include many unique aircraft developed by Wright-Patterson, including the only "Tacit Blue" stealth prototype in existence, which was tested at the famously secretive aviation test site in Nevada known as "Area 51."

ROUND ON THE EDGES:

MILITARY AVIATION

CENTRAL OHIO AEROSPACE TECHNOLOGY CENTER

ALTHOUGH NEWARK Air Force Base officially closed in 1996, parts of its original mission continue under civilian and military management at the site, about thirty miles east of Columbus. About one thousand people, mostly civilian contractors working for Boeing, repair guidance systems here for America's fleet of intercontinental ballistic missiles as well as inertial navigation systems for military airplanes. The Air Force's metrology (calibration and measurement science) facilities on site include a four-level calibration laboratory, possibly the largest facility of its type in the world, built underground to be free from minute vibrations. The primary contractor at the site is Boeing's Space and Communication Group, which operates the Guidance Repair Center. Other parts of the old base continue to be developed for commercial tenants.

RAVENNA ARMY AMMUNITION PLANT

COVERING 21,418 acres, the Ravenna depot is the largest military landscape in Ohio. Like many other military sites in the country, it was established around World War II. Its extensive facilities—located about twenty-five miles east of Akron—manufactured and stored explosives during and after the war, including cartridges, mines, and dynamite. Today, many of the original 623 munitions storage igloos still hold explosives, but weapons assembly at the site ceased in 1992. The nonproduction areas are now used primarily by the Ohio National Guard as a training site for maneuvers involving tanks and aircraft. The most industrialized five thousand acres are slowly being addressed by the military for possible remediation, as the site is heavily contaminated.

ABOUT SIXTY thousand tons of hazardous material—containing lead, mercury, arsenic, and other contaminants—are burned in this incinerator on the Ohio River every year, making it one of the largest of its type in the world. Operated by Von Roll America Inc.'s Waste Technology Industries, it went online in 1993 despite local protests, as it is only eleven hundred feet from a school.

EAST LIVERPOOL WASTE INCINERATOR

ENVIROSAFE CHEMICAL WASTE SITE

OHIO'S ONLY permitted commercial hazardous waste dump sits across the river from Toledo, in the industrial and farming community of Oregon. The site encompasses hundreds of acres of grass-covered mounds and waste-handling sheds. It is one of the nation's only commercial hazardous waste dumps with direct rail access.

MOUNT RUMPKE MEGAFILL

MOUNT RUMPKE is a megafill (one of the nation's largest landfills) in the exurbs of Cincinnati. It was started in 1945 and grows by two million tons of household and industrial wastes per year.
A large landslide occurred in 1996, when the north face of the mound cracked, then slumped downward, churning and exposing fifteen acres of buried waste.
In 2005 the dump was permitted to expand by another three hundred acres, and it's not expected to be declared full until 2022.

BUILT IN 1881, before the age of the automobile, the "oldest concrete street" in America is still in use, outside the courthouse in Bellefontaine, by light traffic only (no trucks are allowed). A statue of the leading proponent for paving the street, a local cement salesman named George Bartholomew, was erected on the site in 1991, the hundredth anniversary of the paving. Although concrete is still utilized in road construction, most American streets are paved with asphalt.

OLDEST CONCRETE STREET

62

ZANESVILLE Y BRIDGE

THIS UNUSUAL bridge, at the confluence of two rivers, has three spans that meet in the middle, enabling travelers to choose between the two shores as their destination. The first version of the bridge was built in 1814. It became part of the National Road, the first federally sponsored "highway," which was commissioned in 1803 and ran from Maryland to Illinois. Portions of the National Road later became the Lincoln Highway, the first continuous, coast-to-coast road in America, which in turn was replaced by the paved Highway 40. Both the Lincoln Highway and Highway 40 passed over this bridge. It was only with the opening of Interstate 70 in the late 1960s, which paralleled much of Highway 40, that the Zanesville bridge ceased to be a landmark on the great American road.

SHENANDOAH CRASH MUSEUM

THE USS *SHENANDOAH* was the first rigid airship constructed in the United States. Built in 1923, it measured 680 feet long. Two years after its maiden flight, it broke apart while airborne during a thunderstorm in southeastern Ohio. Most of the vessel fell to earth near the town of Ava. But the front two hundred feet, borne aloft by helium, traveled another twelve miles before a local farmer tied it to a tree with ropes dropped by crew members who had managed to hang on. Fourteen people died in the crash. The owner of a garage near the crash site converted a camper trailer, recycled from a wreck on the highway, into a museum about the crash.

OHIO STATE REFORMATORY

WHEN IT was built in 1886, at a cost of $1.3 million, the Ohio State Reformatory (also known as the Mansfield Reformatory) was the largest such facility in America. Located midway between Columbus and Cleveland, it evolved over time into a state penitentiary and housed more than 150,000 residents, as many as 3,500 at a time, from death-row inmates to adolescent petty thieves, before closing in 1990. The state built a modern correctional facility next door and began tearing down the reformatory before being stopped by local preservationists. Efforts are under way to restore the building, which is used occasionally as a film location and for ghost hunts. Portraits of Lenin and Stalin loom over the central guardroom, left from the filming of a Harrison Ford feature film, *Air Force One*. Set dressings from *The Shawshank Redemption* are also visible inside.

THIS SITE, one of hundreds of mound locations throughout the Midwest, has been preserved and restored by the National Park Service to showcase what remains of the Hopewell Culture mounds, which were created during a few centuries around the time of Christ. Most of the mounds constructed by Native Americans were destroyed by European settlers, as they were a nuisance to farming and development. Some of the largest mounds and mound complexes, like this one near Chillicothe, were left intact. During World War I, a military base was built on the site, a veritable "city" as well, with two thousand buildings and forty thousand soldiers, an activity that further destroyed many of the mounds.

MOUND CITY

THE WILDS

EXOTIC ANIMALS—including rhinos, giraffes, and camels—roam fourteen square miles of denuded coal-mining lands where the giant crane Big Muskie once reigned. The area, in southeastern Ohio, has been fenced off as a preserve by a conservation consortium that includes zoos and wildlife science organizations. Designed as a research facility for the preservation of endangered species, The Wilds can be visited on "safaris," with tourists loaded onto buses for a closer look at the animals. American Electric Power donated the land for the project.

LONGABERGER IS a privately held, direct-sales marketing company specializing in baskets and traditional home-accent accessories. The firm developed its manufacturing and administrative facilities along Highway 16 in Newark and Dresden as a destination for the consumers of its products, which are sold directly to customers at home through a sales force of seventy thousand independent sales associates. The most prominent of these attractions is the corporate headquarters, where five hundred people work within a seven-story building shaped like one of the company's signature products.

LONGABERGER BASKET COMPANY

DUBLIN CORN FIELD

THE 109 giant ears of corn on a lawn in an office park near the town of Dublin were conceived by the artist Malcolm Cochran in 1994 for the Dublin Arts Council. The installation comments on the transition of much of Ohio's landscape from farms to suburbs. The site, once owned by an agricultural researcher who hybridized corn, sits across the street from a new Nationwide Insurance Company office, where fifteen hundred employees were recently relocated from downtown Columbus, a city with one of the nation's highest downtown vacancy rates.

ROUND ON THE EDGES:

PARTIALLY BURIED WOODSHED

THE ARTIST Robert Smithson conceived and executed this piece, intended as an illustration of entropy, while he was a visiting artist at Kent State University in January 1970. Smithson had a backhoe dump dirt onto an empty shed until the center beam of the wood-and-stucco structure cracked. Upon completion, the installation was officially transferred to the university and valued at ten thousand dollars. At the time, Smithson said he expected the piece to just "go back to the land." Today its remains are hidden in a grove of trees, most of which were planted some time ago to obscure the ruin. The grove is surrounded by the new Liquid Crystal Materials Science building, a football field, and a parking lot.

CAMPBELL HILL

THE HIGHEST point of land in Ohio is Campbell Hill, northwest of Columbus, which tops out at 1,549 feet above sea level. Structures atop the hill are former defense radar facilities, left from the period of 1951 to 1969, when the site was used as part of the nationwide NORAD system to detect enemy aircraft. Radar data from this site were relayed to an operation center in Battle Creek, Michigan, and then to the command bunker inside Cheyenne Mountain, Colorado. The base was converted into the Hi-Point Career Center, a civilian technical school, in 1974.

ANOTHER WAY TO GET YOUR MIND AROUND A PLACE IS TO SHRINK THE WORLD DOWN TO A WORKABLE SIZE, TO GET THE EDGES INTO VIEW. MODELS, MAPS, GLOBES, AND OTHER STYLIZED REPRESENTATIONS OF THE EARTH (OR PORTIONS OF ITS SURFACE) ALL BELONG TO THIS PHENOMENON OF TERRESTRIAL MINIATURIZATION. FROM MODEL RAILROADS TO CARTOGRAPHY, THESE REPRESENTATIONS CAN SAY A LOT ABOUT HOW WE SEE, OR WANT TO SEE, THE WORLD.

The three largest hydraulic models in the world stand as unrivaled monuments of miniaturization. Built by the U.S. Army Corps of Engineers, each one is an engineering marvel and a relic from the end of the analog era. These functional models of waterways are vast, handmade miniature landscapes with flowing water, simulating the fluid dynamics and physical form of the largest and most complex water systems in the United States: the Chesapeake Bay, the San Francisco Bay/Sacramento River Delta system, and the Mississippi River.

They represent both a triumph and a failure of engineering hubris, technological mastery, and terrestrial manipulation. Overshadowed by the digital age, the models are long since obsolete. Today, one is abandoned in place, one is destroyed, and one, the smallest, is maintained primarily as a spectacle for tourists. But even in these various conditions, the model landscapes reflect much about how we, collectively, imagine the world to be and how it often ends up differently.

WOODROW WILSON BRIDGE, ON THE CHESAPEAKE BAY MODEL, MARYLAND

MISSISSIPPI BASIN MODEL
CLINTON, MISSISSIPPI

THE MISSISSIPPI BASIN MODEL is the largest hydraulic model in the world. It is a 1:2,000 (horizontal scale) model of the entire 1,250,000-square-mile Mississippi River basin area and is located on an eight-hundred-acre rural site outside of Jackson, Mississippi. It was constructed by the U.S. Army Corps of Engineers to model the flood characteristics of the river, in hopes of aiding the design and placement of flood control structures. The two-hundred-acre model, once used to accurately simulate the conditions of the 1952 and 1973 floods, now lies abandoned and degraded to a point beyond repair.

Like many of the nation's ambitious terrestrial engineering projects, the basin model was conceived in the WPA days of the 1930s. Construction started in 1943 with the leveling and grading of the site, which was selected for its relative flatness, availability, and proximity to the Army Corps station at nearby Vicksburg, on the Mississippi River. A prisoner-of-war camp was established on the edge of the site, and three thousand German prisoners of war, primarily from General Erwin Rommel's notorious Africa Corps, were relocated there and enlisted to move an eventual one million cubic yards of earth to create a drainage contour that reflected the surface of the United States, east of the Rockies.

Among the world's river basins, only the Amazon and the Congo exceed the Mississippi River watershed in size. The Mississippi basin drains more than 40 percent of the continental United States, extending from Pittsburgh to western Montana and from Canada to the Gulf of Mexico. As an engineering project, the Mississippi River and its tributaries are the primary

work of the Army Corps of Engineers. Along fifteen thousand miles of river in the basin there are thousands of miles of levees and hundreds of locks, dams, and control structures, most of them built by the Army Corps. Many of these features are re-created in miniature in the model.

For example, these fifteen thousand miles of river are condensed into eight miles of channel. The model's is surface is composed of graded land and fifteen acres of interlocking contoured slabs for the river channels, each approximately twelve feet on a side, resting on top of carefully leveled piles. Underneath the slabs is a system of pipes, ranging in size from thin copper supply tubes to drains that measure sixty inches in diameter. Control houses recorded flow information, which was transmitted by a wired and radio network of sensors, and sent signals to the miniature dams and movable water control structures on the model. Water flow rates were regulated by ridges, scoring, and brass blocks in the river channels. Folded metal screens, cut to the height of miniature trees, represent forested floodplains.

By the time the model was finished in 1966, the automation was complete, and the entire model could be run off a central clock. In the model, one hour equaled 18 seconds, and one day lasted five and a half minutes, shrinking time as well as space.

TERRESTRIAL MINIATURIZATIONS:

TERRESTRIAL MINIATURIZATIONS:

SAN FRANCISCO BAY/ SACRAMENTO RIVER DELTA MODEL SAUSALITO, CALIFORNIA

BUILT IN A FORMER WORLD WAR II shipyard warehouse on the shore at Sausalito, the San Francisco Bay/Sacramento River Delta hydraulic model is a 1.5-acre, 1:1,000 scale model of the largest estuary on the West Coast. The Army Corp of Engineers began constructing the model in 1956 to test the Reber Plan, a large-scale engineering proposal to fill in much of San Francisco Bay and deepen ship channels for defense purposes. In the late 1960s the model was enlarged to cover the Sacramento River Delta—which takes in 40 percent of the state's drainage and includes eleven hundred miles of levees—to study flood control, sediment movement, saltwater intrusion, and pollution effects. The model is maintained today as a tourist attraction and for educational purposes. Although no longer used for research by the Army Corps, it is still partially functional and can be hired for private scientific projects.

The model measures 320 by 400 feet, roughly two football fields in size. It was constructed from 286 five-ton slabs, each individually supported on adjustable screws. The orientation of several of the rivers was altered—some were even folded into labyrinths—to fit them into a smaller footprint inside the warehouse. With the river channel width, length, and water volumes accurately represented, these distortions do not affect the model's accuracy.

Some 250,000 copper tags embedded in the basin of the model help slow down the water and compensate for the ten-times vertical exaggeration. If the vertical scale were 1:1,000, as with the horizontal scale, the water on the model would be

AERIAL VIEW OF THE OLD MARINSHIP SHIPYARD,
WHICH EVOLVED, AFTER WORLD WAR II, INTO
SAUSALITO'S RECREATIONAL AND RESIDENTIAL
WATERFRONT. THE LARGEST OF THE REMAINING
SHIPYARD STRUCTURES, IN THE CENTER WITH
THE GREEN ROOF, HOUSES THE SAN FRANCISCO
BAY/SACRAMENTO RIVER DELTA MODEL.

so shallow it would be nearly immeasurable. Though large in area, the San Francisco Bay is shallow, two-thirds of it less than eighteen feet deep.

The model runs about one hundred times faster than nature. In one minute of operation, it demonstrates the equivalent of one hour and forty minutes of model time. Similarly, fifteen minutes equals one day, and three and a half days equals a year.

Sensors on the model monitored salinity (by conductivity), velocity, temperature, and water level, feeding information to a central computer system that was installed in 1983 and upgraded over the years. The ocean, modeled to seventeen miles outside the Golden Gate, was maintained at a salinity of 33 parts per thousand, like that of the Pacific. Dye, confetti, and plastic balls were used to study circulation patterns, captured with video and time-lapse photography for later analysis.

The model has recently aided in the location of bodies from one of the nation's favored suicide locations, the Golden Gate Bridge. By re-creating the tidal and flow conditions present at the witnessed time of death, the search area for the victim can be narrowed significantly. The FBI has also used it to acquire evidence in homicide cases.

TERRESTRIAL MINIATURIZATIONS:

CHINA BASIN

TERRESTRIAL MINIATURIZATIONS:

TERRESTRIAL MINIATURIZATIONS:

CHESAPEAKE BAY MODEL
MATAPEAKE, MARYLAND

THE CHESAPEAKE BAY HYDRAULIC MODEL covered eight acres, making it the second largest hydraulic model in the world and the largest one contained entirely indoors. Like others, the handmade model presented a landscape in miniature. It was built to mimic the largest and most complex estuary system in the country, the Chesapeake Bay, located a few hundred yards beyond the warehouse doors. Though conceived in the 1960s and shut down in the 1980s, the model was operational for only three years, from 1978 to 1981, during which time it generated mountains of data—much of it on digital tape, disks, and printouts that were left in the model's offices and control rooms when the model was abandoned.

Construction began in 1973 and continued until 1977. The surface of the eight-acre model re-created forty-four hundred square miles of land and waterway, at a horizontal scale of 1:1,000, and was hand-sculpted in wet concrete, using Masonite templates as guides. From experience, the Army Corps knew that vertical exaggeration was required for an operable model, so the vertical scale was ten times larger than the horizontal: 1:100. But still, because the bay is so shallow, the model's vertical component had to be very precisely graded through state-of-the-art surveying techniques, such as laser theodolites. The difference in water surface elevation from the most upstream portion of the model to the ocean was just a few inches. The

TERRESTRIAL MINIATURIZATIONS:

water depth on the model averaged three inches, and the deepest point was twenty-one inches, representing the 174-foot deep "hole" off Bloody Point, at the south end of the island where the model sits.

After construction was completed in 1977, the model underwent more than a year of testing, adjusting, and tuning to ensure that it accurately modeled the real bay. During a test, approximately twenty technicians were required to record data from control points and operate the computers and valves that managed the 450,000 gallons of water that flowed through the model's miniature rivers, ocean, and bays. Salinity was controlled by continuously adding tons of salt in the model's Atlantic Ocean tank.

Extreme temperatures in the warehouse, ranging from freezing to more than 120 degrees, led the model's concrete surface to buckle and move dramatically, causing many reconstruction delays, recalibrations, and reverifications over the model's short operational life.

In 1982 the model was shut down for good. Several new uses for the fourteen-acre metal building covering the model have been proposed and attempted. For a number of years, the National Security Agency used the site for storage. Later, a shrimp farm was partially built inside, with tanks and office trailers installed on the edge of the model (for which much of the Potomac River portion of the model was destroyed). Over the years, the model's surface disintegrated, and the shed that housed the model began to collapse.

TERRESTRIAL MINIATURIZATIONS:

SHRINKING BIG IN A SMALL WORLD

TERRESTRIAL MINIATURIZATIONS:

TERRESTRIAL MINIATURIZATIONS:

By 2005 the site was being converted into a commercial marina, and only a portion of the old warehouse roof was left intact. The remains of the model were torn out, ground up into aggregate, and piled outside for reuse or trucked off site for disposal. Some small broken fragments of the model's concrete stubbornly protruded from the exposed dirt, which, tracked up and puddled, resembled yet another generation of landscape.

TERRESTRIAL MINIATURIZATIONS:

BELOW GROUND THERE ARE WORLDS UNTO THEMSELVES, ISOLATED FROM LIFE ON THE PLANETARY VENEER, LIKE TERRESTRIAL SUBMARINES. BEYOND THE UNDERGROUND WORLD OF BOMB SHELTERS, COMMAND AND CONTROL CENTERS, REDUNDANT-RECORDS STORAGE, AND CONTINUITY-OF-GOVERNMENT BUNKERS IS ANOTHER, MORE ACCESSIBLE KIND OF SUBTERRANEAN SPACE: SHOW CAVES. THESE ARE PREEXISTING, NATURAL CAVES THAT HAVE BEEN DEVELOPED INTO

visitable spaces. They represent a uniquely evolved and colorful vernacular with a surprising consistency, as well as an astonishing variety. They are spaces where America is on display, under the surface.

From the first lantern-led tours through Mammoth Cave in the early 1800s, to the drive-through caves of today, some two or three hundred caves nationwide have been opened to the public (out of more than thirty thousand caves discovered in the United States so far). These caves have been transformed by the interests of tourism and by the fancy of cave owners and promoters.

Most modifications to natural caves are of a practical nature, made to accommodate visitors. New entrances are blasted to allow more convenient access, pathways are installed to allow visitors to move easily along otherwise uneven cave floors, and lighting is installed to make rock formations and pathways visible.

The cave developers who go beyond these basic alterations begin a sort of architectural discourse between the strange natural underground features, and sometimes stranger-still man-made forms. The effect is the creation of unprecedented, and even sublime spaces, reflecting the complex relationship between humans and the rest of the natural world.

CARLSBAD CAVERNS, NEW MEXICO

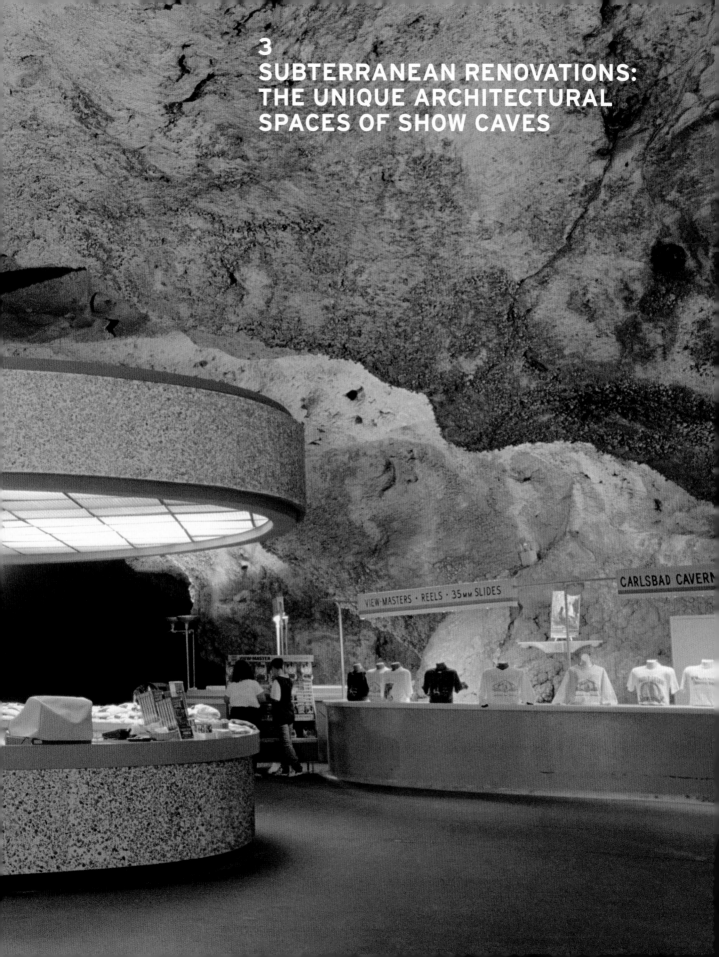

3
SUBTERRANEAN RENOVATIONS:
THE UNIQUE ARCHITECTURAL
SPACES OF SHOW CAVES

ENTRANCE

As the point of transition from the surface to the underworld, the entrance to a show cave can sometimes offer few clues to the character of the spaces below. Jewel Cave, a delicately decorated little gem of a tourist cave in Tennessee, is reached, as in a fairy tale, through a simple wooden door in a hillock overgrown with flowering plants.

Onyx Cave in Kentucky catches tourists off the interstate heading to nearby Mammoth Cave with its large billboard and plain portal. On the hill next to Onyx is a family fun park, with a haunted house and a Ferris wheel. Many smaller show caves have had to add such surface attractions to make up for shrinking attendance in the caves themselves.

Such is also the case at Kentucky Down Under, an Australian-themed animal park/cave attraction. To enter the cave, visitors pass through an unmarked stone arch and descend a stairway that leads down from the asphalt parking lot.

The imposing edifices outside some tourist cave entrances house labyrinths of gift shops and eateries, as at Howe Caverns in New York, the biggest cave attraction in the Northeast.

At Meramec Caverns in Missouri, the entrance and gift shop extend from an external building at the cave's mouth into the natural opening of the cave. The transition is perceptible only by the change of material forming the walls and ceilings of the space, from cement and metal to natural rock. Even the linoleum floor continues far into the cave.

At Carlsbad Caverns in New Mexico, the natural entrance is next to a seating area that resembles a classical Greek amphitheater, where, during the summer months, spectators wait at dusk for hundreds of thousands of bats to emerge. The entrance ramp curves back and forth, descending into the darkness.

Access to Fantastic Caverns in Missouri, the only drive-through cave in the country, is through a metal garage door. At the visitors' center, tourists board specially made wagons, pulled by propane-fueled jeeps, for the ride through the cave.

Elevators have been installed in a number of caves, including Mammoth Cave and Carlsbad Caverns, to manage larger crowds. They also aid in bringing supplies to underground lunchrooms and make access to the caves possible for wheelchair

LIGHTING

The natural cave environment is totally dark, so artificial lighting is needed to make formations visible. Some cave proprietors paint with colored lights, creating multicolored corridors or rooms where a single color washes over the space uniformly. Others employ a warm, white incandescent light that better high-lights varied rock textures.

Light fixtures are often hidden behind existing formations or in coverings made to look like natural features. Concealing wire conduit is considered an art, and professional cave designers gouge troughs in the rock walls or in the cave floor to place miles of wire that may connect thousands of individual fixtures. Wires are covered with a cement mixture made with the natural cave material.

Illuminated panels are often used to highlight geological features and aid in cave interpretation. The names given to individual cave formations are consistent across the country and are surprisingly devoid of mythical or underworld references. Rather, the formations are often said to resemble familiar foods, as with popcorn formations, fried egg formations, bacon formations, and potato chip formations.

Sound-and-light shows, presented in several tourist caves, integrate natural cave formations into a themed spectacle. They usually occur as a climax near the end of the cave tour. At Meramec Caverns, an amphitheater that seats about fifty people has been built overlooking a magnificent wall of flowstone. The lights of the show are controlled manually, responding to a recording of "God Bless America" and culminating in the projection of an American flag onto the natural curtain wall.

Near the end of the tour at Ruby Falls, visitors enter a dark, tall chamber where recorded music builds to an anthemic crescendo; colored lights suddenly turn on to reveal Ruby Falls, a natural waterfall with a veil of water that cascades 145 feet into a shallow pool.

GATHERING SPACE

Dances have been held in caves for many years, especially in caves with nearby populations and in southern states in the days before air conditioning. Stages, bandstands, and dance floors have been constructed and remain in many of these caves. At Meramec Caverns, a rotating mirror ball hangs from the ceiling, and the floor is paved in linoleum tile. Plastic chairs, normally stacked in piles against the wall, are laid out in rows for gatherings of the local Elks Club.

SUBTERRANEAN RENOVATIONS:

The Great Stalacpipe Organ deep within Luray Caverns, Virginia, is a unique and wondrous addition to the natural cave environment. It uses the cave itself as a musical instrument. The organ's keyboard activates padded hammers that strike natural cave formations that were selected for their pitch and tonal qualities, creating resonant sounds like those of crystal glasses being rubbed along their rims, within a three-acre area of the cave. It is billed as the largest musical instrument in the world.

Meetings and performances take place in several show caves, and facilities have been installed to accommodate such gatherings. The Volcano Room at Cumberland Caverns in Tennessee is used for meetings of the National Speleological Society. It's also the site of an annual Christmas party thrown by the cave's operator, Roy Davis, one of the world's only professional cave designers. A three-quarter-ton crystal chandelier, which came from an old theater in Brooklyn, New York, hangs above the meeting area.

Wonderland Cave opened to the public as a nightclub in Bella Vista, Arkansas, a planned resort community built in the Ozarks in the 1930s. Although visitors sometimes toured the expanse of the cave, the primary attractions were the bar, dance floor, and bandstand, where big bands played regularly until the 1940s. In 1931 the Arkansas State Senate held an unofficial meeting in the cave.

SUBTERRANEAN RENOVATIONS:

A bar and nightclub operated in Wonderland Cave until the early 1990s. Now closed, the cave has been heavily vandalized.

Perhaps due to the romantic waterfall-like formations in some caves, or because of their inherent drama, weddings are often held inside show caves. Couples usually state their vows at the base of a large flowstone curtain wall. Some caves cater especially to weddings, such as the beautifully lit Diamond Caverns in Kentucky, where an altar has been installed in an alcove, and Howe Caverns in New York, where a heart-shaped light has been embedded in a brick walkway. The natural chapel at Bridal Cave in Missouri, which features a boat dock on the Lake of the Ozarks, has been the site of more than thirteen hundred weddings.

SUBTERRANEAN RENOVATIONS:

A room inside Truitt's Cave in Missouri is sometimes used as a wedding chapel and reception area. The room contains a working fireplace, which is usually kept burning in the 55-degree cave, even when it is a humid 100 degrees outside in the Ozark summer. The room once held a restaurant where trout, raised in an underground pool in the back of the cave, were served to paying customers. Indeed, food service is another activity that has led to the creation of some interesting subterranean renovations.

The Snowball dining room at Mammoth Cave serves baked goods, drinks, and cold sandwiches from behind a stainless-steel counter. Diners eat nearby at rows of picnic tables arrayed beneath a low natural ceiling of bulbous cave formations called snowballs. The facility stopped serving hot lunches recently when an algae forming on the ceiling of the cave was attributed to heat and steam from the kitchen.

Lunch has been served 750 feet below ground in Carlsbad Caverns since around 1927. Counters were first installed in the 1930s, and the serving facilities have been expanded and improved several times. The current kiosk layout and design was built in 1976. The concession that has held the contract for Carlsbad Caverns for years, the Cavern Supply Company, designed and operates this vending area in the cave. Fried chicken is no longer prepared in the cave, and a blackened part of the cave ceiling is attributed to a kitchen fire some years ago.

In the lunchroom area, several kiosks offer tourist souvenirs, such as View-Master reels and t-shirts. It's also possible to mail postcards and make payphone calls from this part of the cave. Recent efforts to procure funding to remove the lunchroom and vending facilities at Carlsbad have so far failed. The motivation for destroying these unusual facilities is partly due to economics, as the sale of sandwiches has apparently slumped. A desire to project a more responsible stewardship of the cave may also be fueling the movement to restore the lunchroom area (including the removal of the cement floor) to a more natural-looking state.

Of course, if food is made available, so must bathrooms be. Mammoth Cave and Carlsbad Caverns, both of which are owned by the National Park Service and offer lunch, also provide underground bathrooms. These facilities are adjacent to the lunchroom, where their typically institutional ceramic tile work merges into the natural rock walls and ceilings. Sewage is pumped hundreds of feet to the surface.

UNDERGROUND
CLASSROOM

CIENCE
SEARCH
ROGRAM

CAVE ECOLOGY

An increasing sensitivity to cave ecology is changing the way caves are presented and developed. At Fantastic Caverns, school children learn about cave ecology in an underground classroom; a video on the subject is also presented at the turnaround point of the cave tour, where it is projected onto a screen for a captive audience, sitting in tourist carts pulled by jeeps. In fact, the drive-through format is said to decrease visitors' impact on the cave by keeping them grouped in carts and controlling their movements.

Ozark Underground Laboratory in Missouri is a show cave developed to educate the public about the interconnectedness of groundwater in limestone regions. Visitors also learn about the delicate ecology of the cave, which is home to such rare organisms as blindfish, salamanders, cave crickets, and albino crayfish.

Designed by groundwater hydrologist Tom Aley, tours of the cave are conducted by flashlight. The guide (often Aley himself) walks ahead, scanning the gravel path for any creatures that might have wandered into harm's way.

Lost River Cave and Hidden River Cave in Kentucky are two show caves that feature many of the past, present, and possible future attributes of show caves. The first development of Lost River Cave came from industry, as the river flowing into the cave was dammed to power a nearby mill. Mammoth Cave, Carlsbad Caverns, and many other caves that evolved into show caves were also first developed for industry. Some were used to mine bat guano for fertilizer, while the nitrate-rich soil in other caves was a source of saltpeter, a component in gunpowder.

Later at Lost River, the cave mouth was developed into a dance hall, and the surface area outside the cave was turned into a resort. Tours were also led into the cave, and artificial lights were installed, as well as a statue of Jesse James. (Many cave operators, especially in the South, claim that the famous outlaw had a hideout in their cave.) As the nearby town of Bowling Green expanded and industrialized, pollutants seeped into the ground and found their way (due to the drainage characteristics of limestone landscapes, or karst regions, as such porous bedrock landscapes are also called) into the Lost River, and the cave. The cave became so polluted that the EPA has twice declared it a Superfund emergency cleanup site, and tourism has virtually vanished.

Hidden River Cave, located in downtown Horse Cave, Kentucky, also became a toxic waste site, as polluted groundwater backed up into the cave to the point where the odor of sewage (and gasoline from leaking underground gas tanks) made walking on Main Street unpleasant. The cave has recently been cleaned up and is now open again to visitors, who descend a wooden walkway into the cave while hearing about cave ecology and the groundwater dynamics of karst regions.

At street level, the American Cave Museum has displays about these matters; it is also the headquarters for the American Cave Conservation Association. In the visitors' center, a two-story, man-made grotto of plaster cave formations gives visitors a sense of the splendor of show caves, but without the cave at all; the cave experience has been reduced to symbolic and didactic interpretations.

A balance between these two extremes—the well-intentioned reductions of the preservationist and the distracting interventions of cave developers—is perhaps unattainable. But a most sublime show cave experience can be had by just wandering unescorted in a well-lit cave, allowing one's mind to wonder upon the transformations we impose on mysterious places in order to feel at peace with the wild, natural world.

THE SHASTA DAM UNDER CONSTRUCTION, 1944

4
UNDER WATER: INTENTIONALLY DROWNED TOWNS

HUNDREDS OF TOWNS LIE BURIED BENEATH THE WATERS OF ARTIFICIAL LAKES AND RESERVOIRS ACROSS THE UNITED STATES. THEY SAY THAT BEFORE THE FLOODING, THE LAND WAS CLEARED, BUILDINGS WERE REMOVED, AND THE DEAD WERE REBURIED ON HIGHER GROUND. BUT THE ERASURE IS NEVER COMPLETE—MUCH REMAINS SUBMERGED.

It's impossible to remove history, despite how much we forget. The fact is that these towns were there, that people lived in homes along these streets. These are the ultimate ghost towns. They were sacrificed for the perceived needs of the majority, cast aside the path of progress. Created by force, they linger, at times like a bad conscience, like the shadow of a collective inequity.

The following six towns represent a generalized, regional, and submerged history of this country: from the native settlements of the Great Plains through the mining era in the West, the growing dominance of New York City, the establishment of the mill towns of New England, and the New Deal industrialization of the South to the continuing explosive growth of the arid Southwest. The nation's story is embedded beneath the surface, and at times it emerges to remind us of what was—and to intimate what will be.

THE FLOODED PLAIN

ELBOWOODS, NORTH DAKOTA, IS SEEN FOR THE LAST TIME IN THESE AERIAL PHOTOGRAPHS TAKEN ON JULY 7, 1953, AS THE FLOODWATERS OF NEWLY FORMED LAKE SAKAKAWEA APPROACHED THE CENTER OF THE EVACUATED TOWN.

ELBOWOODS WAS ONE OF SEVERAL NATIVE AMERICAN TOWNS along the Missouri River that were permanently flooded following the completion of the Garrison Dam in North Dakota in 1953. The town was established in 1891 as the local headquarters for the region's Hidatsa, Mandan, and Arikara tribes. By the 1950s, though still populated entirely by Native Americans, the town looked and functioned like a typical rural American town of a few hundred people. Elbowoods had gas stations, stores, and a post office, as well as the reservation's main school and hospital. The lake that formed behind the Garrison Dam was named after Sacagawea, the legendary

Shoshone Indian woman who guided Lewis and Clark through the mountains of Montana. Built by the U.S. Army Corps of Engineers, the dam flooded a quarter of the Fort Berthold Indian Reservation, forcing the relocation of 325 families, nearly 80 percent of the population. Many moved to a newly established community called New Town, where fifteen hundred members of the Three Affiliated Tribes now operate a large casino.

Stretching two hundred miles, Lake Sakakawea is the third-largest reservoir in the country. It was made primarily to control flooding and silting on the commercially navigable portions of the Missouri River far downstream, between places like Sioux City, Omaha, Kansas City, and St. Louis. From its headwaters near Yellowstone Park in the Rocky Mountains to its terminus at the Mississippi in St. Louis, the Missouri is North America's longest river, cutting deep into the Great Plains. When steamboats first made it this far up the muddy and meandering waterway in 1819, the fur traders who piloted them set off their cannons to further astound the stunned natives watching from along the banks. Since then, the river, once full of snags, sandbars, and other obstacles, has been nearly totally engineered and dammed.

BOOMTOWN SUNK

THE SHASTA DAM IMPOUNDS LAKE SHASTA,
IN NORTHERN CALIFORNIA

THE OLD MINING TOWN OF KENNETT was still home to a hundred people when it was flooded by Lake Shasta in 1944. Like other "gold rush" towns in northern California, it was established for mining and prospecting in the region in the 1850s. The population began to rise substantially after a railroad camp was built in 1883, with more than a thousand Chinese laborers. Gold was discovered nearby the next year, and a post office came in 1886. The largest copper smelter on the West Coast opened in Kennett in 1905, and by 1911 three thousand people lived in town. Acid fumes from the smelter exfoliated and denuded the surrounding hills, and farmers in the valley fifteen miles away sued its operator for destruction of their crops. The mines and smelter closed after World War I, and Kennett's population fell over the next two decades. The town now rests beneath four hundred feet of water, as do many of the region's smelters, paint factories, and mines.

INTENTIONALLY DROWNED TOWNS

Originally called the Kennett Dam, as it is located next to the old townsite, the Shasta Dam is the second-largest concrete dam in the nation (after the Hoover Dam) and the last of the big Depression-era federal dam projects. It was built by the Bureau of Reclamation between 1938 and 1945 as the cornerstone of the Central Valley Project, an effort to control the Sacramento River. By holding back much of the winter rains in the Lake Shasta reservoir, it made water available to farmers during the dry summer months, when it was most needed. The project's vast distribution network stretched throughout the Central Valley of California, where more than half of the nation's food and fiber is now grown.

132   UNDER WATER:

*LAKE SHASTA SLOWLY RISES IN DOWNTOWN
KENNETT, CALIFORNIA, FLOODING THE MEAT
MARKET, BOARDING HOUSE, POST OFFICE,
AND GOLD NUGGET CAFE, LATER SET AFLAME
BY THE BUREAU OF RECLAMATION.*

INTENTIONALLY DROWNED TOWNS

Neversink, N. Y.

NEVERSINK (whose fateful name is said to be derived from the Indian word "ne-wa-sink," meaning "continuously flowing") was the larger of two New York communities that were removed in 1942 to make way for a reservoir. The other town was called Bittersweet. A total of 340 people were evicted from the valley, and 6,149 acres were condemned. Some buildings were relocated to nearby towns, but most were bulldozed and burned in a "final harvest." Trees were removed, cellars were filled in, privies were disinfected, and barnyard manure was even said to have been dug up to maintain New York City's reputation for having the finest-quality drinking water possible. Flooding began on June 4, 1953, and the reservoir took two years to fill.

UNDER WATER:

GOTHAM'S THIRSTY REACH

*PRE-DAM POSTCARD VIEW OF THE TOWN OF
NEVERSINK, NEW YORK, REMOVED DURING THE
CONSTRUCTION OF THE NEVERSINK DAM, FOR
THE CREATION OF THE NEVERSINK RESERVOIR.
THE TOWN WAS ONE OF DOZENS THAT HAVE
BEEN PERMANENTLY STRUCK FROM THE MAP
TO ENABLE NEW YORK CITY TO GROW.*

The eight million residents of New York City consume more than a billion gallons of water per day. As demand has increased, the watershed for the city has extended 120 miles upstate in a series of leaps that started in the nineteenth century and ended (for now) with the completion of the Delaware Aqueduct system in 1965. The Delaware system includes four reservoirs— Cannonsville, Pepacton, Rondout, and Neversink—that are connected by nearly two hundred miles of underground tunnels ten feet in diameter. It supplies half of New York City's water.

Twelve communities were removed to make way for the other three reservoirs, displacing 3,457 people. Two other water supply systems serve New York City. The adjacent Catskill Aqueduct system (built between 1907 and 1927), comprised of the Ashokan and Schoharie Reservoirs, supplies another 40 percent of the city's water. And the older Croton Aqueduct system (built between 1837 and 1911) supplies the remaining 10 percent. In all, thirty-six towns have been lost for New York City's water, with more than ten thousand people displaced.

*THE TOWN OF NEVERSINK SITS MORE THAN
ONE HUNDRED FEET BELOW THE SURFACE,
JUST BEHIND THE DAM.*

INTENTIONALLY DROWNED TOWNS

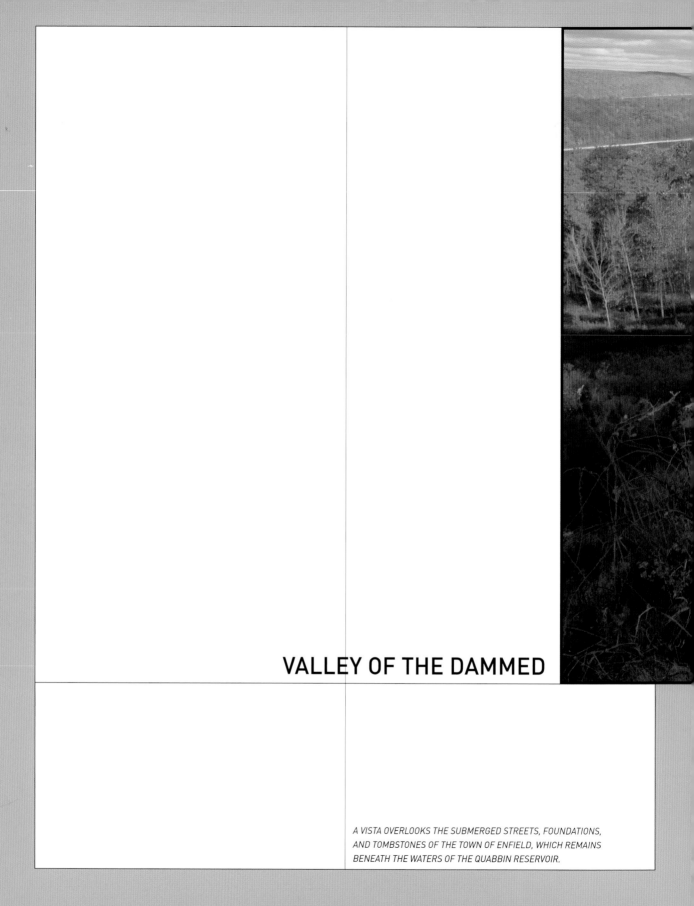

VALLEY OF THE DAMMED

A VISTA OVERLOOKS THE SUBMERGED STREETS, FOUNDATIONS, AND TOMBSTONES OF THE TOWN OF ENFIELD, WHICH REMAINS BENEATH THE WATERS OF THE QUABBIN RESERVOIR.

Enfield Overlook

The two photographs above, together with the vista before you, represent a vivid chronology of this place called Quabbin.

The top photograph was taken in 1927. It provides an excellent panoramic view of the town of Enfield which, along with the towns of Dana, Greenwich, and Prescott plus several smaller villages, was discontinued in March, 1938, to allow for the construction of this vast drinking water supply reservoir.

The lower photograph was taken during 1939, after Enfield was dismantled. Throughout the entire Swift River Valley, no buildings of any kind were standing when the reservoir began to fill in August, 1939. Several of the structures in the top photograph may still be seen, however, in sites to which they were removed in communities surrounding Quabbin.

The only physical evidence of Enfield remaining before you now are the terraces of the former Woodlawn Cemetery, on the easterly side of Mt. Ram, near the water's edge. The former Enfield business district lies under 90 feet of water.

As you view the vastness of Quabbin and its watershed, pause and reflect upon what this uprooting has meant for those who once called these lands their home. Keeping these lands and waters pure protects the values of Quabbin for water supply and also keeps the trust of those who left the valley so that it could be used for this purpose. Further information on the history of Quabbin Reservoir and its management is available at the Quabbin Visitor Information Center at Winsor Dam.

THE SCENIC NEW ENGLAND VILLAGES of Dana, Prescott, Greenwich, and Enfield were all disincorporated on the same day, April 28, 1938. Over the next year, the valley was demolished and deforested by more than a thousand "woodpeckers," immigrant workers from Boston who at times ran amok in the doomed landscape, living in the vacated houses along the Main Streets, and burning churches without authorization. Some old buildings were moved to other towns, but most were bulldozed into piles and burned, as were thirty square miles of forest. The valley was on fire for months. In all, twenty-five hundred people were relocated. Seven thousand bodies from local cemeteries were reinterred on higher ground. The Quabbin Reservoir finished filling in 1946. It has no flood control, electrical generation, or navigation functions. It was built for one purpose only: to serve the drinking water needs of Boston, sixty miles away. Still considered the largest single-purpose reservoir in the nation, it is the city's primary water source.

Forty thousand acres of land around the reservoir are owned by the state and controlled by the Metropolitan District Commission of Boston, and access is highly limited. The dozens of islands—former hilltops protruding from the water—are off limits to the public, as is the largest landmass in the reservation, the Prescott Peninsula, where the remains of most of the town of Prescott lie overgrown in the woods. A radio astronomy observatory has been constructed there to take advantage of the remoteness and silence in an otherwise densely populated state.

DIVERS RECENTLY DISCOVERED MANY REMAINS OF TOWNS ALONG THE SWIFT RIVER, INCLUDING FOUNDATIONS, FENCEPOSTS, GARBAGE DUMPS, OUTFALL PIPES, AND CEMETERY PLOTS.

THE DEEP SOUTH

THE TOWN OF BUTLER, TENNESSEE,
BEFORE THE FLOOD

BUTLER WAS ONCE THE COMMERCIAL CENTER
of the Watauga Valley in eastern Tennessee. With a population
of around six hundred, it was the only real town in the region.
It was a typical southern town, with two barbershops, two beauty
parlors, markets, the Blue Bird Cafe, a hardware store, a drug-
store, a few service stations, a few hotels, three churches,
a rail station, a Masonic lodge, a brick City Hall, a bank, and
doctors' and dentists' offices. Located in the forested hills
of Appalachia, Butler was also home to wood-related industries
such as a lumber company, a crating company, a furniture
company, and a casket company. When the floodgates were
closed in 1948, the Watauga Dam and Reservoir began flooding
458 square miles along the Watauga River and displacing 735
families. About 175 buildings, including shops, barns, churches,
and homes, were moved to higher ground, to a new townsite
named New Butler. Most buildings were demolished on site, and
twelve hundred bodies were moved from the graveyards, but
some families opted to leave the graves of their ancestors undis-
turbed. So they are still there, along with a reported slave graveyard that crews from the Tennessee Valley Authority never found.

When engineers emptied the reservoir to service the dam in 1983, Old Butler re-emerged after thirty years beneath 150 feet of water. Former residents toured their hometown for the few weeks that it was exposed. Don Stout's shoe store, made of stone, and the one-room jailhouse, made of concrete, stood out from the other foundations and building pads along the muddy streets, still lined with trees, long dead but preserved by the water.

The Tennessee Valley Authority, a government entity established during the Depression, has engineered watersheds in seven states, electrifying and industrializing the rural South. It's now the largest energy producer in the United States, having constructed dozens of power plants and hydroelectric dams, like Watauga, since its inception. Butler was the largest single community, and the only incorporated town, removed by the Tennessee Valley Authority throughout the entire massive public works project. The agency expects to draw down Watauga Lake again around 2015, exposing Old Butler to a new generation of descendants of former residents.

UNDER WATER:

BUILDINGS, ROADS, AND WALLS ARE AMONG
THE REMAINS OF THE TOWN OF BUTLER THAT
WERE EXPOSED FOR A FEW WEEKS DURING A
DRAWDOWN OF THE RESEVOIR IN 1983, BEFORE
BEING SUBMERGED AGAIN.

INTENTIONALLY DROWNED TOWNS

145

DRAUGHT AND DROUGHT

THE FORMER TOWN OF ST. THOMAS, NEVADA, normally lies up to sixty feet below the surface of Lake Mead. But regional droughts cause extreme fluctuations in southwestern reservoirs, and St. Thomas has appeared and disappeared five times since it was abandoned sixty-five years ago. Each time it reemerges, more of it is gone.

Like most early settlements in the desert Southwest, St. Thomas was established in an area of available water, in this case the comparatively lush Moapa Valley, fifty miles

EXPOSED REMAINS OF ST. THOMAS, BRIEFLY BAKING IN THE NEVADA SUN

northeast of where Las Vegas is now. The town started as a Mormon outpost in 1865 and was later part of a chain of agricultural communities along the Muddy River—including Moapa, Logandale, and Overton—which cut through the arid terrain. St. Thomas's population peaked at around five hundred people. For a while the town was known for producing cantaloupes and asparagus. A railway spur served the valley, and U.S. 91 (the main highway to Los Angeles before Interstate 15 was built) went through town, making it a stop for motorists. In 1938, however, as Lake Mead crept northward, filling in behind the Boulder Dam, St. Thomas, located at a lower elevation at the southern end of the valley, was flooded. Today portions of forty buildings are visible at the exposed remains of St. Thomas, including the old school and the Hannig Ice Cream Parlor. Also visible is the foundation of the Gentry Hotel, where President Herbert Hoover stayed in 1932 while inspecting the nearby construction project he had helped to create. The Boulder Dam, which flooded the town, was later renamed in his honor.

Lake Mead is the nation's largest reservoir, and the Hoover Dam is the nation's tallest dam. Like most big dams and reservoirs across the United States, they are products of the Great Depression's need for jobs and the desire to help a growing population develop and settle new land. In the Southwest, these federal projects provided electricity and reliable water sources, enabling cities to grow in an otherwise impossible place. As the country's population center moves south and west, pulled by the rapid development of desert cities like Phoenix and Las Vegas, the limits of these artificially supplied resources will continue to be tested. A reminder of a subtler riparian past, the shrinking ghost of the small agricultural community of St. Thomas will continue to reappear, the hotter and drier it gets.

UNDER WATER:

INTENTIONALLY DROWNED TOWNS

ANOTHER VERSION OF AMERICA CAN BE FOUND IN SITES THAT PLAY OTHER PLACES FOR TRAINING PURPOSES. THESE REPRESENTATIVE LANDSCAPES ARE DISTILLATIONS OF PORTIONS OF THE WORLD, AND AS THIS ERA OF PREPAREDNESS PROGRESSES THEY ARE INCREASING IN SOPHISTICATION AND OCCURRENCE ACROSS THE COUNTRY. THEY ARE AN EXPRESSION OF HOW EMERGENCY PLANNERS, POLICE, FIRE, AND MILITARY PERSONNEL INTERPRET THE TOWNS, STREETS, AND LANDSCAPES IN WHICH WE LIVE.

The scenario grounds for emergency training in Southern California include mock hazardous material spills, train wrecks, building collapses, fires, and debris-strewn landscapes. Police trainees contend with civil decay, robberies, hostage situations, looting, riots, and snipers in mini–Main Street environments called situation simulation villages, tactical training sites, or "Hogan's Alleys," where live weapons or small dye-filled rounds (known as simunition) lend realism to the scenario. Whether they are made for police or fire departments, these training sites are stylized versions of ordinary places, with the extraordinary horrors of the anticipated future played out on a routine basis. In Southern California, where these sites are juxtaposed with the prop towns and back lots of the Hollywood scenery makers, training villages and emergency props range from the typical to the state-of-the-art.

5
PRACTICELAND:
PLACES PLAYING PLACES

COLLAPSED-BUILDING TRAINING STRUCTURE,
DEL VALLE TRAINING CENTER, CALIFORNIA

LOS ANGELES POLICE DEPARTMENT ACADEMY

ONE OF THE EARLIEST TRAINING TOWNS still in use in the Los Angeles area is the situation simulation village at the Los Angeles Police Department Academy in Elysian Park. The academy is the department's longtime classroom and firearms training area. It was established in the late 1920s as a private shooting range for officers and has served as the depart- ment's main training campus for more than fifty years. Although they have long been staffed by LAPD employees, the grounds and the buildings are still owned by the private Los Angeles Police Revolver and Athletic Club.

The academy grounds feature a swimming pool, a café, a dining club, a rock garden, a gymnasium, an athletic field,

PRACTICELAND:

INTERIOR AT THE SITUATION SIMULATION VILLAGE

THE SITUATION SIMULATION VILLAGE AT THE LAPD ACADEMY

classrooms, three firing ranges, two electronic simulation training rooms, and two outdoor tactical training areas. The situation simulation village, sometimes referred to there as the "SIT-SIM village," is on a hillside near the rock garden. It was built in 1975 with help from Universal Studios volunteers. It consists of a series of connected facades with individual doors. The rooms are also linked by interior doorways, enabling a continuous search scenario to be played out from one end of the complex to the other. Props inside are minimal, and the building is fairly simply constructed. Only simunition rounds—high velocity mini-paintball bullets—are used in this facility.

*TARGET IN TACTICAL TRAINING
CENTER ALLEY*

*BISECTED CAR PROP IN TACTICAL
TRAINING CENTER ALLEY*

Another training scenario site at the police academy, located between two shooting ranges, is the practical combat range at the Tactical Training Center. This is a small Hogan's Alley with a number of corridors that terminate at fixed and moving targets. Unlike the SIT-SIM village, this is a live-fire range, with a large bullet trap consisting of piles of shredded tires, faced by a painted rubber mat. It was improved and modified following the notorious 1997 North Hollywood shootout, in which heavily armed and well-armored bank robbers alarmed police with their firepower.

MAILBOX SHOWING BULLET-HOLE SIZES

PLACES PLAYING PLACES

155

ED DAVIS
TRAINING FACILITY

ANOTHER MAJOR LAPD SITE is the Edward M. Davis Emergency Vehicle Operations Center (EVOC) and Firearms/ Tactics Training Facility, located next to the 405 Freeway in Granada Hills. Opened in 1998, it is the department's newest and most elaborate training facility. Much of the grounds is occupied by 4.4 miles of track used to teach driving techniques.

One of only two large EVOCs in Southern California, the Ed Davis facility has two skid pans, a collision avoidance simulator, an inner-city street grid, blind driveways, sharp turns, elevation changes, and a high-speed track. The 137,000-square-foot main building houses electronic driving simulators, offices, classrooms, firing ranges, and a maintenance garage for EVOC vehicles.

PRACTICELAND:

THE SITUATION SIMULATION VILLAGE AT THE LAPD'S ED DAVIS FACILITY

HOUSE AT THE SITUATION SIMULATION VILLAGE

BANK INTERIOR

*BANK AT THE SITUATION
SIMULATION VILLAGE*

Located between the main building and the EVOC is the most postmodern civilian tactical training village in Southern California. The situation simulation village has a gas station, a bank, a bar, a convenience store, a hotel, a house, and a coffee shop. The village is used by recruits, by officers for advanced training, and for the production of training videos. Trainees use simunition rounds and wear face shields and vests for protection. The interior walls of the buildings are coated with vinyl, making it easier to wipe off the multicolored simunition splatter.

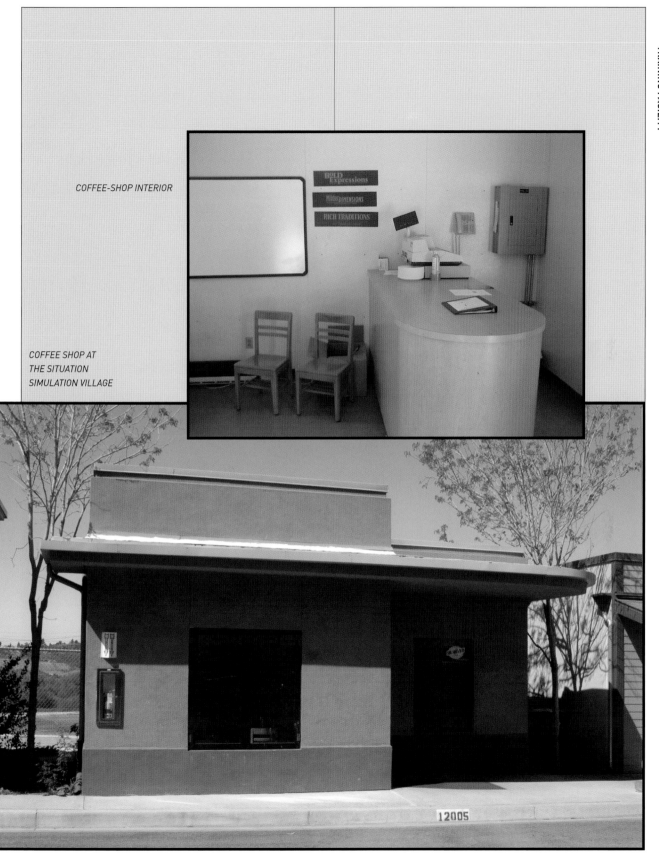

COFFEE-SHOP INTERIOR

*COFFEE SHOP AT
THE SITUATION
SIMULATION VILLAGE*

PLACES PLAYING PLACES

LOS ANGELES SHERIFF'S TACTICAL TRAINING CENTER

LOS ANGELES COUNTY LASER VILLAGE

THE LOS ANGELES COUNTY SHERIFF DEPARTMENT is the largest sheriff's department in the world, with more than 14,000 employees (8,500 sworn, 5,800 civilian). One of its major locations is City Terrace, a former garbage mound east of downtown Los Angeles that has been developed into a county complex. In addition to shooting ranges, fire-training facilities, correctional facilities, and emergency command centers, the county operates its only active training simulation village, which is still referred to as a "laser village," though the laser-based training weapons were replaced with simunition-firing weapons several years ago.

The village consists of a shopping plaza–type structure, with a second floor and balcony, and an adjacent home and garage. The main building was constructed in the 1980s for this purpose, and rests on the asphalt with no foundation. Although still in use, it was recently condemned by county building inspectors for being structurally unsound. The building has a simulated bar, a liquor store, an escrow company office, a check cashing store, a hotel, a drive-up ATM, and a women's medical clinic.

PRACTICELAND:

*PART OF THE LOS ANGELES SHERIFF'S SHOPPING PLAZA,
OFFICE, AND RESIDENTIAL PROP BUILDINGS IN THE
LASER VILLAGE, STILL IN USE, THOUGH OFFICIALLY
CONDEMNED BY THE COUNTY BUILDING DEPARTMENT*

T'S CHECK-CASHING SERVICE

DRIVE-UP ATM

MEDICAL CLINIC

PRACTICELAND:

*OFFICER-DOWN DUMMY ON THE FLOOR, LITTERED
WITH SIMUNITION ROUNDS, IN THE HOTEL BUILDING
AT LASER VILLAGE*

ORANGE COUNTY
TACTICAL
TRAINING CENTER

THE SHERIFF'S DEPARTMENT OF ORANGE COUNTY operates one of the state's most realistic simulated police training villages, the Tactical Training Center. Located in the city of Orange, the center trains thousands of officers, agents, and private security company employees from the western United States. Like the Los Angeles County Sheriff's tactical village at City Terrace, Orange County's Tactical Training Center was built as a laser village in the 1980s, when practice weapons emitted a laser light and "victims" wore vests that electronically detected the approximate strike of the beam. Now small dye-filled simunition pellets are used.

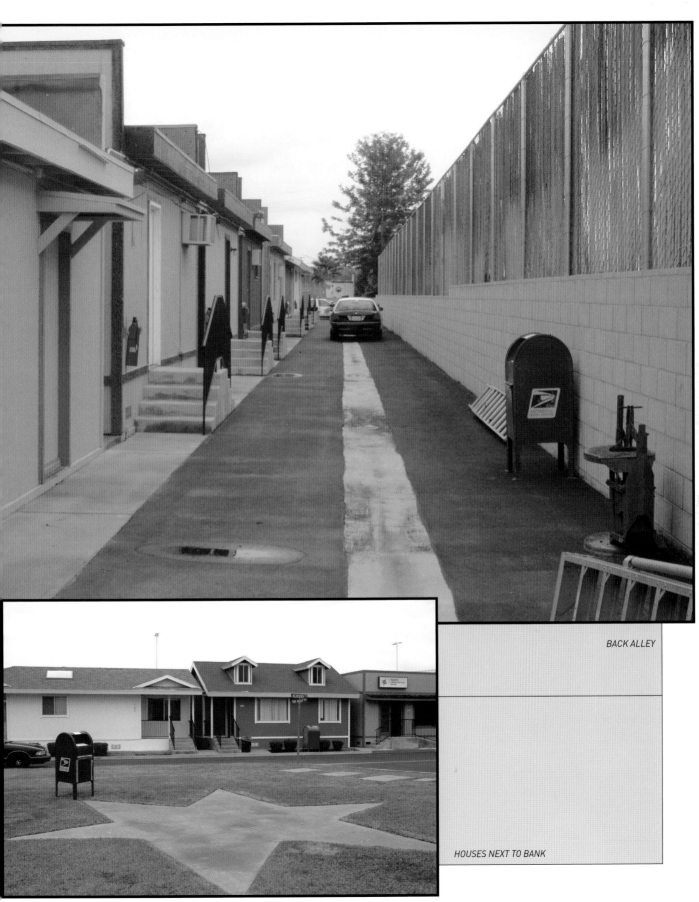

BACK ALLEY

HOUSES NEXT TO BANK

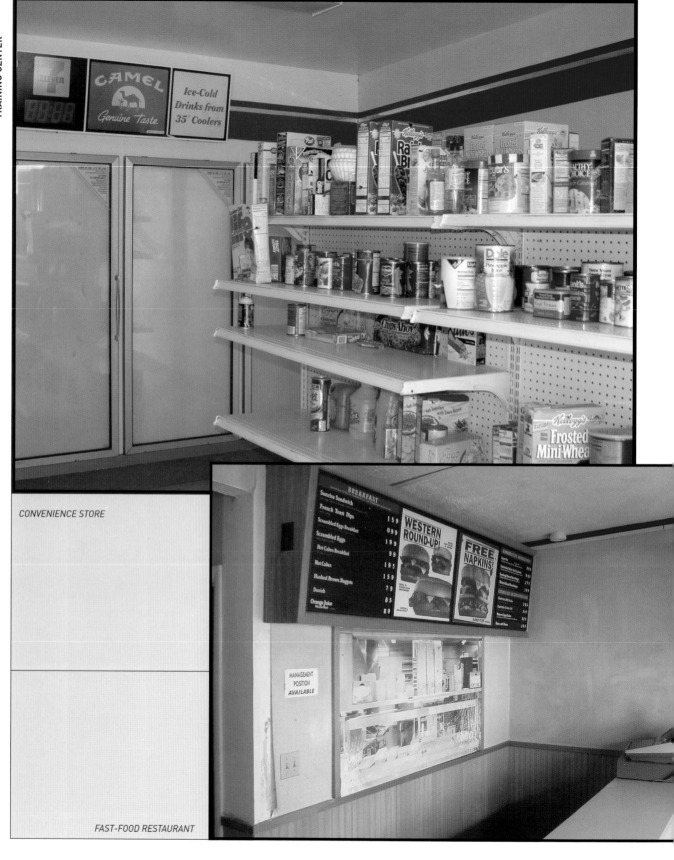

CONVENIENCE STORE

FAST-FOOD RESTAURANT

PRACTICELAND:

CONVENIENCE STORE BACK ROOM

HOUSE INTERIOR

The village has eight buildings: three residences, a convenience store, a bank, a bar, a fast food restaurant, and a
service station. Though the buildings are smaller in area than
their real counterparts, realism is heightened by the use
of actual commercial signs and props. In scenarios involving
building searches, ambush survival, bomb squad training,
bank robberies, hostage situations, and sniper confrontations,
live actors play roles such as store clerks and customers.
The five simulated businesses are in fact sponsored by the companies themselves, which support their maintenance through
donations to police community foundations.

*VIEW FROM THE OBSERVATION TOWER
AT THE SAN BERNARDINO COUNTY'S EMERGENCY
VEHICLE OPERATIONS CENTER*

SAN BERNARDINO COUNTY EVOC

THE SHERIFF'S DEPARTMENT OF SAN BERNARDINO COUNTY, east of Los Angeles County, operates what may be the largest dedicated EVOC in the nation, a seventy-eight-acre site that opened in 1991. In California, the only such facility approaching it in size and diversity is the forty-three-acre EVOC at the California Highway Patrol's training site outside Sacramento. Unlike that facility and the Ed Davis EVOC in Los Angeles, the San Bernardino County EVOC is a single-purpose facility, not part of a larger training site. It sits on a dusty plain, next to a wash and an off-highway vehicle recreation area, south of Glen Helen. Police departments from all over the country send their training officers here for instruction.

PRACTICELAND:

SIMULATED RAIL CROSSING

SUBURBAN ROAD GRID

The center has a mile-long high-speed track, a large skid pan made of polished concrete that, when watered, becomes as slick as ice. A large asphalt lot in the middle of the track is primarily used as a motorcycle obstacle course. It also has a residential street grid with numerous intersections, a few four-wheel-drive obstacle courses, and a simulated rail crossing. Overseeing it all is an observation tower atop the administration and classroom building. The San Bernardino County EVOC has a fleet of several dozen cars, including some that have been especially modified to practice the PIT maneuver (short for Pursuit Immobilization Technique), a police tactic for nudging cars into a skid.

PRACTICELAND:

FOUR-WHEEL-DRIVE OBSTACLE COURSE

MOTORCYCLE OBSTACLE COURSE

PLACES PLAYING PLACES

171

FRANK HOTCHKIN
MEMORIAL
TRAINING CENTER

THE FRANK HOTCHKIN MEMORIAL TRAINING CENTER is the main crew training site for the City of Los Angeles's fire department. It is located near Dodger Stadium, and occupies the structures and grounds of a former Marine Corps Reserve Center. It is named after a firefighter who died while battling a blaze at the building that, a few years later, would become the department's fire training headquarters.

172

THE FIVE-STORY METAL DRILL TOWER
AT THE FIRE DEPARTMENT'S HOTCHKIN
TRAINING CENTER

*DRILL TOWER
BURN-ROOM CONTROL*

ROOF-TRAINING PROP

The outdoor training areas contain what may be the largest rooftop-training prop in Southern California. It is a structural skeleton of a building, with a large flat-roof area and a tall pitched-roof area. Firefighters practice shoring and cutting through roofing and flooring material, something often done in fighting structural fires to vent gases and smoke and to prevent potential flashovers. Also on site is a five-story metal drill tower, which was recently ordered from a company that premanufactures them and then assembles them on site. This drill tower has "hot house" capability, meaning that portions of it can ignite with propane to create more realistic training conditions.

PRACTICELAND:

SHIPPING-CONTAINER RESCUE HOUSE

SALVAGED VEHICLES
FOR VICTIM EXTRACTION

PLACES PLAYING PLACES

175

ACCESS ROAD

FIRE-EXTINGUISHER TRAINING AREA

DEL VALLE
TRAINING CENTER

THE FIRE DEPARTMENT OF LOS ANGELES COUNTY operates five training sites: the department headquarters and command center on Eastern Avenue, known as "the Hill" (next to the sheriff's complex); an eastern training center in Pomona, used for recruit training; a northern training site in Lancaster, with the county's only active live-fire tower; a classroom site in La Quinta; and the Del Valle Training Center near Castaic, the largest and most diversified fire-training site in the Los Angeles region.

Del Valle is located on a hilltop and uses 160 acres of land that the county bought from Unocal in 1984. Much of the focus of Del Valle is technical rescue training. There are industrial props (including a portion of an oil refinery), vehicle accident props (including propane-powered bus collisions), construction site accident props, confined space rescue props, and other urban search and rescue facilities. There is also a hazardous material training area with railcars and a chemical storage building and a fire extinguisher training area.

PRACTICELAND:

*BUS ACCIDENT
PROP AREA*

CONFINED-SPACE AND TRENCH TRAINING AREA

HAZMAT AREA TANKER-TRAILER PROP

SHORING TRAINING BUILDING

CONFINED-SPACE TRAINING STRUCTURE

CONSTRUCTION-SITE SHORING TRENCH

NORTH NET
FIRE TRAINING CENTER

THE NORTH NET TRAINING SITE in Anaheim is operated by a consortium of cities in northern Orange County. It's used by fire departments from Southern California as well as from out of state. Built in 1978, it was the most elaborate fire training center in Orange County until the Regional Fire Operations and Training Center in Irvine opened in 2005.

The main feature of North Net is a five-story concrete training tower with propane-fueled fire capability, also used for ladder and rope rescue training. The tower is surrounded by such fire-training basics as door-breach props, roof ventilation props, and wood for shore construction training. South of the tower is an area where trainees learn to cut concrete and lift and move heavy objects, as well as tunnels and tubes where they practice rescues in confined spaces. Junked cars are regularly delivered to the site to be used for cutting and for victim-extraction training.

PRACTICELAND:

HEAVY-OBJECT-LIFTING TRAINING PROP

PRACTICELAND:

CONCRETE-CUTTING TRAINING

VICTIM-EXTRACTION TRAINING REMNANT

PLACES PLAYING PLACES

DERAILED RAIL-CAR PROP

VENTURA COUNTY FIRE TRAINING CENTER

JUST NORTHWEST OF LOS ANGELES COUNTY lies the increasingly urbanized Ventura County, which has an elaborate regional training center on the edge of Camarillo Airport. The site is operated by the Ventura County Fire Department, which has several significant structures for rescue training, firefighting training, and hazmat response training. These facilities include several climbing and rappelling props, including a five-story tower (for urban search-and-rescue drills), an elaborate confined-space rescue tunnel network, two simulated roof structures, and an electrical transmission system prop.

The hazmat training area is especially advanced and is used by fire departments and law enforcement agencies from Ventura County and beyond. Its training scenarios simulate hazardous tanker and rail car accidents and spills, industrial tank leaks, and a methamphetamine lab, which is built inside a shipping container and situated in a miniature orange grove.

PRACTICELAND:

CONFINED-SPACE AND SHORING TRAINING CENTER

PLACES PLAYING PLACES

185

CLANDESTINE DRUG LAB WITH HAZMAT TRAINEE

ELECTRICAL UTILITY TRAINING AREA

PRACTICELAND:

ROOF-AND-FLOOR-STRUCTURE TRAINING PROP

CALIFORNIA SPECIALIZED
TRAINING INSTITUTE

LIKE MANY CITY AND COUNTY AGENCIES, the state also operates training sites for emergency personnel and police. The Office of Emergency Services of the State of California operates a multifaceted training site called the California Specialized Training Institute. It exists to train law enforcement, emergency management, and other first responders in emergency procedures and tactics, including responses to earthquakes, terrorism, and hazardous material spills. It is located on the grounds of Camp San Luis Obispo, a large National Guard training base in the mid-coast of California. The institute maintains several training areas with different functions, including the only "mock emergency operations center" in the state, where disaster scenarios are played out in a fictional disaster town called Santa Luisa Del Mar, which was modeled after Santa Barbara but with the addition of a harbor.

MOCK TOWN VIEW

LEAKING TANKER-CAR PROP

PLACES PLAYING PLACES

GAS TANK PROPS

BACK ROOM OF EMERGENCY OPERATIONS CENTER
SHOWING MAP OF SANTA LUISA DEL MAR

PRACTICELAND:

A SIMULATED METHAMPHETAMINE
LAB AT THE INSTITUTE

A portion of Santa Luisa Del Mar has been assembled in three dimensions for police scenario training using simunition, with buildings recycled and relocated from other parts of the base. Other training areas at the institute include a large and scattered hazmat training yard with prop rail cars brought in from actual derailment sites. The institute's criminal justice program has developed one of the open shooting ranges on base with some structural props, used for live-fire weapons training. The Department of Toxics and Substance Patrol has created what is probably the most elaborate mock clandestine drug lab ("clan lab") in the state. Prisoners from a state penitentiary across the highway were brought in to decorate the space.

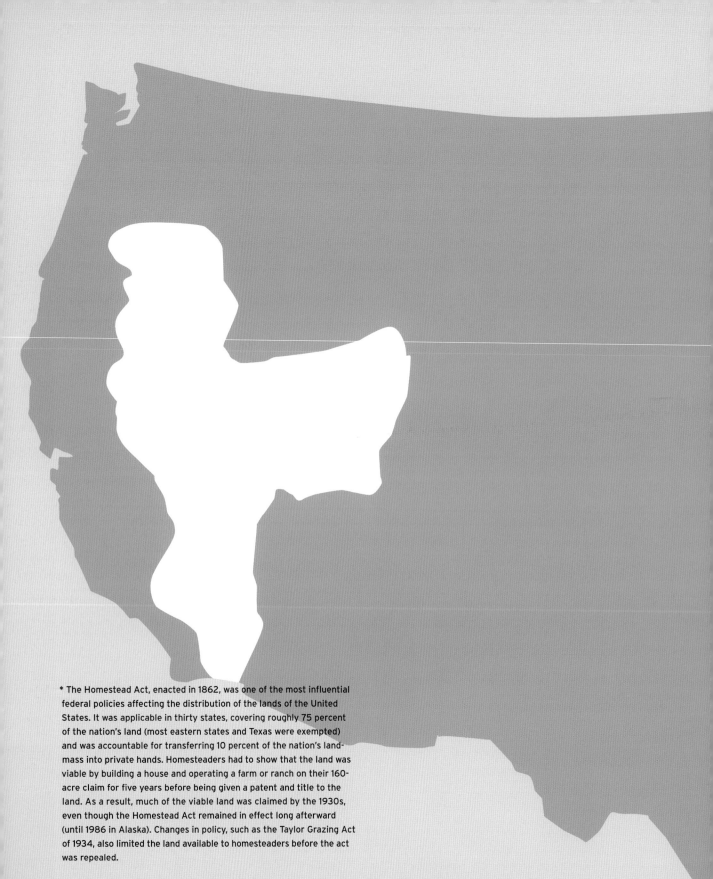

* The Homestead Act, enacted in 1862, was one of the most influential federal policies affecting the distribution of the lands of the United States. It was applicable in thirty states, covering roughly 75 percent of the nation's land (most eastern states and Texas were exempted) and was accountable for transferring 10 percent of the nation's land-mass into private hands. Homesteaders had to show that the land was viable by building a house and operating a farm or ranch on their 160-acre claim for five years before being given a patent and title to the land. As a result, much of the viable land was claimed by the 1930s, even though the Homestead Act remained in effect long afterward (until 1986 in Alaska). Changes in policy, such as the Taylor Grazing Act of 1934, also limited the land available to homesteaders before the act was repealed.

6
FEDERALAND: AMERICA'S INTERNAL FRINGE

THE GREAT BASIN REGION POSES SPECIAL NOTIONS OF LIMINALITY, OF SELF-CONTAINMENT, AND OF ISOLATION. IT IS A DESICCATED HOTHOUSE OF AMERICA'S EXTREMES. PHYSIOGEOGRAPHICALLY, THIS IS A DISTINCT ZONE WITHIN THE UNITED STATES, COVERING MUCH OF THE STATES OF NEVADA AND UTAH, AND PORTIONS OF CALIFORNIA, OREGON, AND IDAHO. IT IS A NETWORK OF WATER-SHEDS WITH NO OUTLET TO THE OCEAN. IT IS THUS DISCONNECTED FROM THE CIRCULATORY SYSTEMS OF THE WORLD. THE REASON FOR THIS HYDRAULIC

isolation is dryness. The rain that falls in the basin evaporates before the basin can fill up and spill over into other water-sheds that flow to the ocean. Whatever falls within it, stays within it. It has no away. In many respects, it *is* away. This great landscape bowl has become an internal margin.

This is also the largest concentration of land outside Alaska that is owned by the federal government, specifically the Department of the Interior, and more specifically the Bureau of Land Management. The BLM inherited the land that was left over when the Homestead Act was repealed for the lower forty-eight states in 1976.* This was the land that couldn't even be given away. The BLM was established in 1946, but its mandate for these federal lands did not shift from disposal to retention until 1976. The agency, now responsible for 8 percent of the nation's landmass—including half of the

desert land in California, 44 percent of the state of Utah, and 86 percent of Nevada—is directed by Congress to manage this land in a way that will "best meet the present and future needs of the American people." So the BLM is in the middle of all the demands made on the Great Basin.

On a map, Federaland is sort of heart-shaped, but it functions more like another part of the anatomy. It captures much of the waste stream and has more large-scale NIMBY (Not In My Back Yard) land uses than anywhere else. It may be that anatomical place, an away place, and a "negative" space, but it is a whole lot more as well, including a reflection of national systems of defense and industrial production. Though it is not in most of our back yards, it is in all of our back yards—our collective American back yard. And the Great Basin, as we know, has no drain.

MILITARY RANGES

Land use, like nature, does not favor vacuums, and the Great Basin has filled up with things that are drawn to emptiness. Within the basin are the largest military practice lands in the world, making it one of the most shot-at and bombed places on earth. Some of these landscapes (many of them larger than some eastern states—and not just Rhode Island) double as test ranges for some of the most dramatic, experimental, and high-impact technologies in the world. In addition to restricted military areas totaling more than ten thousand square miles, there are thousands of square miles of public land that are officially suspected of having unexploded ordnance left over from earlier days of training.

BOMBING DEMONSTRATION ON THE NELLIS RANGE

THE NELLIS RANGE, north of Las Vegas, is both the nation's largest restricted area and its busiest Air Force bombing and training range. Fighter pilots from Nellis Air Force Base (at the opposite end of Las Vegas Boulevard from the casinos on the Strip) train here in twelve thousand square miles of "special use" airspace over forty-seven hundred square miles of restricted land in southern Nevada. To support war games, the range uses fixed and mobile threat-simulators, simulated enemy airfields,

mock industrial facilities, radar stations, and telemetry facilities. Target objects, such as tanks and aircraft, are set up for inert and live bombing practice, and portions of the range are wired for electronic warfare training. Also within the range are several large-scale complexes with distinct functions and histories, including the base at Groom Lake (known popularly as Area 51), a "secret" Air Force base that is known as the development, test, and evaluation site for numerous advanced aircraft and weapons systems. At the north end of the range is the Tonopah Test Range, managed by the Department of Energy's Sandia National Labs and used for weapons testing and development, including, recently, earth-penetrating bombs. On the west side of Nellis is Indian Springs Auxiliary Field, which the Department of Defense uses as a base for unmanned aerial vehicles.

IF THE AIR FORCE DOMINATES southern Nevada, the Navy, based out of the Fallon Naval Air Station, has the skies over the northwest part of the state. Here fighter pilots train on the Navy's largest network of bombing and electronic scoring ranges, a complex of five separate ranges within sixty miles of one another, clustered around the main base at Fallon. Bravo 16, Bravo 17, the Wilson Range, Bravo 19, and Bravo 20 are used for bombing and strafing runs, with live and dummy ordnance, and for electronic warfare training. Together the ranges comprise about one hundred thousand acres. Classrooms at the main base at Fallon are linked electronically to the ranges, allowing real-time monitoring of training activities in the field. Fallon is the home for the Top Gun academy, which moved there from Miramar Naval Air Station in California (now a Marine facility).

BRAVO 17 IS ONE OF FIVE RANGES USED BY THE NAVY IN NORTHERN NEVADA.

A PUBLIC ROAD PASSES THROUGH THE MIDDLE OF UTTR'S NORTHERN AREA, ON THE WAY TO A REMOTE PENINSULA ON THE GREAT SALT LAKE.

are coordinated through Hill AFB, near Ogden, Utah, forty miles away from the range by air. UTTR's grounds are bisected by the Interstate 80 corridor, which runs east-west from Nevada to Salt Lake City. The area south of the interstate includes the Wendover Bombing and Gunnery Range, with more than a million acres of secured land in military use since World War II. Also in the south area is Dugway, which is considered part of UTTR although it is also the Army's chemical and biological weapons testing area. Oasis is the primary on-site support facility for the UTTR, located in the north range, about fifteen miles from Interstate 80. The 388,000-acre northern area handles most of the testing activities, conducted mostly by a test group out of Edwards Air Force Base. According to an Air Force representative, "Just about every munition out there has been tested at the UTTR."

THE UTAH TEST AND TRAINING RANGE (UTTR) is a large military area in northern Utah, with portions contiguous and overlapping with Dugway Proving Ground. It has more than 19,000 square miles of restricted airspace and 2,675 miles of ground space, making it the nation's largest combined restricted land and closed special-use airspace area (Nellis has more land, but UTTR has more sky). On the ground, numerous target areas, radar, and video facilities support more than twenty-two thousand training sorties and one thousand test sorties annually. Missions

THE LARGEST OF SEVERAL BOMBING RANGES at the southern end of the hydrographic Great Basin is the Chocolate Mountain Aerial Gunnery Range, a 456,000-acre restricted area on the east side of the Salton Sea, in Southern California. The Navy and Marine Corps use it for aerial gunnery and bombing practice, primarily for aircraft based out of the Marine air station in Yuma, Arizona, and the Navy base at El Centro. Navy SEALs also practice desert warfare tactics on the range. It is administered by the Yuma Marine Corps Air Station.

PRACTICE BOMBS DROPPED ON THE RANGE ARE COLLECTED BOTH BY THE MILITARY AND BY SCRAPPERS, WHO SNEAK ONTO THE RANGE LOOKING FOR VALUABLE METAL PARTS TO SELL TO RECYCLERS.

THE ROAD CONNECTING FORT IRWIN
TO THE HIGHWAY IS A ROAD
THROUGH NOWHERE, TO SOME PEOPLE.

FORT IRWIN, northeast of Barstow, California, is one of the Army's largest and busiest training ranges. Infantry live and train in battlelike conditions here in long-term desert warfare scenarios. Tanks, personnel carriers, and helicopters are used in full-scale simulated battles, where the home force act as the enemy against visiting infantry from other bases around the country. The thousand-square-mile range is wired for electronic battle simulations using lasers instead of live munitions.

AT THE SOUTHERN END of the Great Salt Lake Desert lies one of the nation's most mysterious and unusual field test sites, Dugway Proving Ground. Dugway is the nation's primary chemical and biological weapons testing and training site and it combines the microscopic world of its chemical and biological laboratories with large-scale testing and training outdoors. The land within Dugway's eight hundred thousand secured acres of Utah desert is dotted with several industrial and military complexes and is latticed with overlapping target ranges and dispersal grids. The grounds of Dugway are used primarily by the Army and Air Force for smoke and obfuscant testing, chemical and biological weapons training, detonation and dispersal research, and other weapons and projectile experimentation. Further uses of the facility have included chemical weapons disposal research, nuclear reactor meltdown tests, and cosmic ray studies at the Fly's Eye observatory. Although Dugway has used live biological and chemical agents in open-air tests on its ranges in the past, current field training is done with "simulants"—inert materials with characteristics similar to dangerous agents, according to official reports. Live agents are used in tests in several laboratory facilities at Dugway.

ONE OF SEVERAL RADIATING
TEST GRIDS AT DUGWAY

CHINA LAKE, in the northern part of California's Mojave Desert, is a vast weapons development facility and testing range. Almost every munition in the Navy's arsenal has been tested within this facility, which encompasses more than a million acres, or 1,723 square miles. Numerous laboratories and test ranges, located mostly in the north area of China Lake, support weapons development. In the southern portion of the reservation are electronic ranges that support training and weapons proving. China Lake is part of the Navy's Western Test Range complex, along with White Sands in New Mexico and Point Mugu, a base on the Southern California coast. Missiles are launched from Point Mugu to ranges in the Pacific Ocean, as well as over land to impact points at China Lake and White Sands.

CHINA LAKE IS THE NAVY'S MAIN AIR-GROUND WEAPONS TESTING SITE.

MORTAR PRACTICE RANGE AT THE TWENTYNINE PALMS COMBAT CENTER

THE NATION'S LARGEST Marine Corps facility, the Twentynine Palms Marine Corps Air-Ground Combat Center, is also in the Mojave portion of the Great Basin, between the Chocolate Mountains and Fort Irwin. Within the area's 932 square miles, military training and weapons testing are performed in association with other branches of the armed forces. Fifty thousand marines train at the Twentynine Palms Combat Center every year. The base has more than a thousand structures, most located in the community of Mainside, and employs about eleven thousand military and civilian personnel.

FEDERALAND:

THE COMPASS ROSE ON ROGERS DRY LAKE, THE HEART OF EDWARDS AIR FORCE BASE, IS MORE THAN A MILE WIDE.

EDWARDS AIR FORCE BASE, in the Mojave Desert north of Los Angeles, is an active Air Force base that serves the aeronautic defense industry through several facilities on the 301,000-acre secured base. Much of this facility is located on the western edge of Rogers Dry Lake, a naturally flat, forty-four-square-mile landing area for experimental aircraft. Edwards is primarily known for its history of flight testing and experimental-aircraft evaluation. It's where Chuck Yeager broke the sound barrier and where just about every aircraft in the U.S. military inventory has been tested. Flight tests at Edwards take place in the skies above the base and surrounding public land and at ranges all over the Southwest. Edwards employs about ten thousand people at its Air Force, Army, and NASA facilities. Within the perimeter of Edwards are bombing areas with wrecked aircraft and live ordnance.

MUNITIONS MANUFACTURE, STORAGE, MAINTENANCE, AND DISPOSAL

The region is not just a playground for munitions; it is their nursery and graveyard as well. Explosive and propellant production plants have clustered in the isolation of the Great Basin, though even here the suburbs are encroaching. Vast fields of storage igloos contain millions of rounds in all shapes and sizes, some new, and some old and unstable. Those that are obsolete or destined for disposal in accordance with international treaties are detonated, immolated, or incinerated on distant hillsides or in remote valleys.

THIS PLANT HAS E
THE COMMANDING
DIRECTIVE ISSUED
1954. PURSUANT
ACT OF 1950. UN
VEHICLES ENTERI
MAKING NOTES, D
AREA OR ITS ACT
BY THE COMMANI
POSSESSION OF U

PERIMETER SIGNAGE
AT THE HAWTHORNE DEPOT

THE LARGEST WEAPONS STORAGE and disposal site is the Hawthorne Ammunition Depot in western Nevada, a 147,000-acre base with 2,427 munitions storage igloos. An estimated 75 percent of them are in use. Also on site is the Western Area Demilitarization Facility, a sixty-eight-million-dollar,

STRICTED AREA
WARNING
ECLARED A RESTRICTED AREA BY AUTHORITY OF
CER IN ACCORDANCE WITH THE PROVISIONS OF THE
HE SECRETARY OF DEFENSE ON THE 20th. OF AUG,
E PROVISIONS OF SECTION 21 INTERNAL SECURITY
RIZED ENTRY IS PROHIBITED. ALL PERSONS AND
REON ARE LIABLE TO SEARCH. PHOTOGRAPHING,
GS, MAPS OR GRAPHIC REPRESENTATIONS OF THIS
S, IS PROHIBITED UNLESS SPECIFICALLY AUTHORIZED
FFICER. ANY SUCH MATERIAL FOUND IN THE
ORIZED PERSONS WILL BE CONFISCATED.

Y
ON PLANT
LIABLE TO SEARCH
R LEAVING THIS
CONSTITUTES CONSENT
STALLATION:
ALCOHOLIC BEVERAGES -
IG OFFICER

thirteen-building complex that processes and recycles outdated munitions; a forty-nine-thousand-acre test range; and a seven-hundred-acre bomb disposal site located twenty-five miles northeast of Hawthorne. Over the years, chemical weapons have been stored and disposed of at Hawthorne, and there are several areas contaminated by mustard gas and other chemical agents. Much of Oregon's Umatilla Army Depot, Arizona's Navajo Army Depot, and New Mexico's Fort Wingate operations were moved to Hawthorne in the early 1990s. Curiously, the Navy's Underwater Nuclear Warfare Center had a location here as well.

ANOTHER LARGE MUNITIONS STORAGE SITE in the basin is the Tooele Depot, a twenty-four-thousand-acre base just south of the Great Salt Lake, which is used to store and dispose of non-nuclear weapons. More than nine hundred munition-storage igloos, spread across the valley floor, provide two million square feet of secured storage space. At the site's western edge is an "open burn" area for disposing of surplus and unstable munitions; open detonations have been known to occur at the rate of two major blasts per day.

ROWS OF STORAGE TANKS KEEP WEAPONS SYSTEMS OUT OF THE WEATHER AT THE TOOELE DEPOT.

ICBMs COME BY RAIL AND TRUCK TO HILL AIR FORCE BASE FROM THE MISSILE FIELDS OF THE NORTHERN PLAINS.

NORTH OF SALT LAKE CITY, near the city of Ogden, is Hill Air Force Base, the nation's primary maintenance and logistics center for ICBMs, such as the Minuteman and Peacekeeper missiles. The facility also specializes in repairing landing gear and installing and maintaining photographic and reconnaissance equipment. It has one of the busiest single runways in the Air Force, with more than eighty-five thousand aircraft operations annually. Hill also coordinates training missions on the Utah Test and Training Range. More than fifteen thousand military and civilian employees work at the 6,698-acre base.

THE DESERET CHEMICAL DEPOT, thirteen miles south of the Tooele Depot, is home to almost half of the nation's chemical weapons. Until a few years ago, nearly thirty million pounds of aging mustard and nerve agents were stored in 208 igloos at the facility, awaiting disposal in accordance with international treaties. Near the igloo field is the Tooele Chemical Agent Disposal Facility incinerator, completed in 1994 at a cost of several hundred million dollars. The controversial disposal plant started burning the chemical weapons at the depot in August 1996. The incinerator is operated by the EG&G corporation, and it is the first of several incinerators the Army may construct at other facilities where chemical weapons are stored.

THE NATION'S ONLY CHEMICAL WEAPONS INCINERATOR IS WORKING ITS WAY THROUGH THE STOCKPILE IN THE RUSH VALLEY OF UTAH.

A STATIC DISPLAY OF SOME OF THE DYNAMIC PRODUCTS MADE AT THE THIOKOL PLANT

MANY OF THE MISSILES, ROCKETS, AND BOMBS that are tested, stored, and disposed of in the Great Basin were made here in the first place. The Thiokol plant, a sprawling and isolated facility near Promontory, Utah, builds ICBM rocket engines and other missile propellant systems as well as rocket motors for the NASA space shuttle. The plant, once designated as Air Force Plant 78, employs more than three thousand people in 450 buildings, clustered in the various industrial and test areas that are scattered throughout the bare hills of the thirty-square-mile complex.

*THE ENTRANCE TO AN ISOLATED
DISPOSAL SITE IN THE
NORTHERN PART OF THE UTAH
TEST AND TRAINING RANGE*

IN THE NORTHERN AREA of the Utah Test and Training Range lies a munitions disposal site and open burn area at Sedal Pass called the Thermal Treatment Unit. Nonnuclear explosives with yields of more than ten kilotons can be detonated here, currently the only facility in the country where disposal of such high-yield ordnance is permitted. The explosions can be heard for miles. Hundreds of Poseidon rocket motors, most taken from the old Hercules facility in nearby Magna, are being disposed of at the Thermal Treatment Unit in fulfillment of START treaty agreements.

ATK, also known as Alliant Techsystems, recently bought the Thiokol plant in Promontory and the former Hercules plant, known as the Bacchus Works, in northern Utah. Bacchus is a munitions, propulsion, composites, and explosives development and manufacturing complex located on a hill surrounded by the suburbs of southwestern Salt Lake City. Among the products produced here are propulsion systems for many types of long-range missiles in the U.S. arsenal. ATK, which spun off from Honeywell in 1990, is now a major defense contractor, with fifty separate facilities in twenty-three states. In fact, it's now the country's largest conventional munitions maker, supplying the Department of Defense with 95 percent of the bullets it uses in training and combat worldwide.

*THE BACCHUS WORKS MUNITIONS
AND PROPELLANT PLANT, WITHIN
VIEW OF THE GREAT SALT LAKE*

NUCLEAR TESTING

Not all of the weapons tested and stored in the Great Basin are "conventional," or nonnuclear. The basin has the largest amount of radioactive land in the country, concentrated around the nation's primary nuclear proving ground in southern Nevada.

THE NEVADA TEST SITE is an 860,000-acre (1,350-square-mile) restricted area owned and operated by the Department of Energy. It is a multi-use, open-air laboratory that was the primary location of the nuclear weapons testing program for the United States and the United Kingdom. Other uses of its grounds include hazardous waste storage, conventional explosives testing, plutonium dispersal tests, nuclear propulsion systems development, and research into remediation technologies. One hundred atmospheric tests have been conducted here, starting with the Able test, a one-kiloton bomb dropped from a bomber above Frenchman Flat on January 27, 1951. The last intentional atmospheric shot, Little Feller I, took place on July 17, 1962. The Limited Test Ban Treaty went into effect the following year, prohibiting testing underwater, in the air, or in outer space, thus forcing nuclear testing underground. And so began the modern era of testing at the Nevada Test Site. At least 921 nuclear charges have been detonated beneath its landscape. The underground testing program created the subsidence craters that pockmark Yucca Flat. Many were performed within excavated cavities and tunnels and on the high ground at the site's northwest corner. Many other forms of "dirty" and land-consumptive research and development have taken place at various locations all over the site, including nuclear rocket engine development programs, hazardous material spill tests, penetrator bomb tests, and seismic tests. Small-scale underground nuclear tests still take place at the site's U1a facility, and explosives tests are conducted at its Big Explosives Experimental Facility, known as BEEF.

*THIS BANK VAULT IS AMONG THE
ICONIC REMAINS FROM ATMOSPHERIC
TESTING ON FRENCHMAN FLAT.*

TWELVE LARGE-SCALE NUCLEAR DEVICES have been detonated on continental land outside the boundaries of the Nevada Test Site—in Colorado, New Mexico, Alaska, and even Mississippi. The Great Basin hosted two of these "off-site" nuclear tests, where the soil underground will remain radioactive for thousands of years, even if the surface is open to the public. One of them, a test called Faultless caried out in 1968, set off a one-megaton underground nuclear explosion to explore the possibility of developing the area as a second nuclear testing location. The Central Nevada Test Site, located fifty miles north of the existing test site, was expected to host several high-yield nuclear tests associated with antiballistic missile systems; however, faulting and slumping of the ground during the first test proved that the area was geologically unsuitable, and the tests were conducted in Alaska instead.

VISIBLE REMNANTS AT THE FAULTLESS SITE INCLUDE AN EIGHT-FOOT-THICK, STEEL-LINED COLUMN WITH AN ATOMIC ENERGY COMMISSION PLAQUE ON IT AND A DRY WASTEWATER POND.

THE OTHER "OFF-SITE" NUCLEAR TEST LOCATION
in the Great Basin is the Shoal test site in northern Nevada.
Conducted in 1963, Shoal was an experiment to study the earth-
quake-like effects of nuclear bombs. A twelve-kiloton bomb (the
one dropped on Hiroshima, Little Boy, was fifteen kilotons) was
detonated twelve hundred feet below the surface. Although remediation work was conducted in the late 1990s, the site remains
unmarked and unfenced. A monument commemorating the test
at the site was destroyed, some say, by Navy pilots from Fallon.

*VISIBLE REMNANTS OF THE SHOAL
TEST SITE INCLUDE REBAR, CEMENT PADS,
AND A CLOSED-OFF SHAFT PORTAL.*

NUCLEAR AND TOXIC WASTE

Waste from nuclear and other hazardous industries across the nation finds its way to the Great Basin, where it is generally collected in lined pits dug by waste disposal companies. As the pits are filled, the disposal cells are covered with earth or crushed rock, creating low-slung trapezoidal mounds that can resemble pre-Columbian pyramids and ceremonial structures. These industrial byproducts can have lives thousands of years longer then the ephemeral goods and services they came from.

ENTRANCE TO THE YUCCA MOUNTAIN REPOSITORY, UNDER CONSTRUCTION

AT YUCCA MOUNTAIN, Nevada, the federal government is trying to develop the largest collection of one of the most deadly substances known to man. Located on the western edge of the Nevada Test Site—on land owned by the Department of Energy, the Bureau of Land Management, and the Air Force—Yucca

FEDERALAND:

Mountain is the only site being seriously considered as a final repository for the nation's high-level commercial nuclear waste: seventy thousand tons of used fuel rods generated over the past few decades by the hundred or so nuclear power plants in the country. A six-billion-dollar program to study the site and partially build the repository has been under way since the early 1980s, but a repository won't open until at least 2010, if ever. The state of Nevada vows that it will not permit it to open. If it does not, the waste may move to interim storage locations, such as the proposed site in the Skull Valley of Utah, also in the Great Basin.

US ECOLOGY, JUST SOUTH OF BEATTY, NEVADA

UP THE ROAD A FEW MILES

from Yucca Mountain, south of the town of Beatty, is one of the few commercial waste sites in the country that can accept hazardous waste that is also radioactive. Operated by a company called US Ecology, this is the final repository for such "mixed" wastes as radioactive polychlorinated biphenyls from plants nationwide. It opened in 1970 as a radioactive waste site and has a capacity of more than one million cubic yards. The permitted radioactive storage functions have now reached capacity, and the site no longer accepts radioactive waste. It just has to keep what it already has isolated for the coming millennia.

THE ENVIROCARE FACILITY in northern Utah is the largest of the few commercial facilities in the nation that can accept mixed radioactive and hazardous wastes, and unlike US Ecology, it is still active. Envirocare has greatly expanded since 1986, when it was opened by the Department of Energy for the disposal of uranium mill tailings. It now accepts radioactive material from most of the department's major industrial sites, from commercial generators, and from military sites.

RADIOACTIVE FRAGMENTS OF THE DEPARTMENT OF ENERGY PLANT AT OAK RIDGE, TENNESSEE, AWAIT BURIAL AT ENVIROCARE, IN UTAH.

DOWN THE ROAD FROM ENVIROCARE, sharing part of a development zone that has been designated as the West Desert Hazardous Industries Area by Tooele County, are two major hazardous waste incinerators. The one at Clive is now closed and up for sale. The other, at Aragonite, receives waste from industrial sites across the country and burns a minimum of thirty thousand tons of solvents, paints, old chemicals, contaminated soils, and polychlorinated biphenyls (PCBs) every year.

*THE REMOTE
HAZARDOUS
WASTE
INCINERATOR
AT ARAGONITE*

*NORTHEAST CORNER OF THE
GRASSY MOUNTAIN WASTE SITE*

ACROSS THE HIGHWAY FROM ARAGONITE, and a dozen miles into the distance, is a square mile of land known as the Grassy Mountain hazardous waste site. This is a final resting place for the ash left over in Aragonite's incinerator and for toxic materials, such as PCBs and asbestos, from all over the country.

SALT/WATER

Although it's generally considered desert and contains the largest flat spaces in the hemisphere, the Great Basin is anything but uniform in its topography. Much of it is "basin and range," a rippling sequence of mountains and valleys, aligned longitudinally from east to west, from the Rockies to the Sierras. The extreme degree of oscillation includes the highest peaks in the Lower 48—more than fourteen thousand feet high—and the deepest valleys in the nation, plunging to over two hundred feet below sea level. From the "greatest snow on earth" to the badwaters of Death Valley, there are hundreds of lakes in the basin, including some of the largest in the nation, but most are dry mud.

THE BIG EXCEPTION IS THE GREAT SALT LAKE, the vast puddle of the Great Basin. It is the largest body of water in the country after the Great Lakes and the saltiest body of water on earth after the Dead Sea. The lake is, in a way, on the edge of existence itself. Few people recreate on it or even visit its shores. The only creatures that live in it are brine shrimp, harvested seasonally by a strange industry of fishermen in specialized boats; their catch is mostly packaged and shipped overseas to be consumed by fish in Asian fish farms. The lake often seems to slip in and out of perceptibility, its waters merging invisibly in the horizon's sky. Sometimes the lake appears indistinguishable from the mirages that occur around its gently sloping shores. The lake is a stubborn remnant of the desiccated Pleistocene Lake Bonneville, once hundreds of feet higher, and covering much of Utah, until a postglacial, prehistoric natural dam broke in the north, and the lake drained cataclysmically into Idaho's Snake River basin, through the Columbia, and out to sea. That was the last time the Great Basin drained. Since then, the lake has slowly shrunk to the point it is at today. Its water level fluctuates as much as twenty feet in as many years, reflecting the relative imbalance between evaporation rates (as high as six feet per year) and local precipitation and snowmelt. Like an exaggerated

barometer of regional weather patterns, the lake reached a historical peak in 1986 (4,212 feet above sea level), causing flooding of railways, roads, and real estate, and prompting the state to build a battery of pumps on its western shore to pump it out into the salt flats to the west. Then a drought began, and in 2004 the lake reached its lowest level (4,193 feet above sea level) since the early 1960s.

THE GREAT SALT LAKE'S NORTHEASTERN SHORE

*A CRUMBLING RESORT ON THE
WESTERN SHORE OF THE SALTON SEA.
IT HAS SINCE DISAPPEARED.*

MEANWHILE, the flooding of the other large body of water in the hydrographic Great Basin seems to have stopped. The Salton Sea, in the southeastern corner of California, is a forty-mile-long inland sea formed by accident. It's now a briny agricultural sink in one of the most arid places in the country. Before the sea formed, the area was a dry depression, below sea level and north of one of the state's most productive agricultural areas. In 1905, an irrigation canal that brought Colorado River water to the valley was overwhelmed by high water from rains along the Colorado watershed. The entire flow of the Colorado River drained into the Salton Sink, rapidly filling it up with water, before the breach could be dammed. Now the sea is a wet dump for the salty water washed off the agribusiness fields of Imperial Valley, possibly the most productive agricultural area in the nation. The gradual flood of agricultural water, which had been ruining seaside real estate schemes for decades, has been controlled by the irrigation district and the state, and the sea's surface seems to have stabilized at around 228 feet below sea level. Now the sea is just contending with its diminishing water quality and increasing salinity.

DRIP-WATERING FEEDERS IRRIGATE SALT GRASS ON THE DRY LAKE BED, AS PART OF THE DUST MITIGATION EFFORTS ON OWENS LAKE.

AT THE OPPOSITE EXTREME IS OWENS LAKE, famously dried up by the creation of the Los Angeles Aqueduct. The aqueduct, finished in 1913, tapped the streams and rivers that fed the lake. By the mid-1920s, its crusty, flaky, and dusty lake bottom was exposed to the air, becoming the nation's largest point source of inhalable particles and a health risk for downwinders. Eighty years later, the Los Angeles Department of Water and Power has been persuaded to address the dust problem by installing a five-hundred-million-dollar system of shallow flooding and vegetation, covering the most emissive thirty square miles of the one-hundred-square-mile lake bed. It remains to be seen if the project, initiated in 2001, will be effective, though locals say it has improved conditions for stinging insects.

THE MOUNTAINS ERODE AND MELT into the rivers and washes of the Great Basin, but instead of washing away into the pluming deltas of America's great rivers, these sediments terminate at pluvial lakes, forming deposits of mud sometimes thousands of feet thick. This mud contains the finely ground and mixed constituents of the entire landscape, a full spectrum of minerals, metals, chemicals, and compounds. Dry lakes—and even wet ones—are the source of some unusual industrial sites in the basin. The sediment of Searles Dry Lake, located in the isolated southern end of Panamint Valley, is said to contain traces of nearly all known elements, and has been mined for several decades by local industries. The IMC Chemical Company is the current operator of the mining and processing complexes around the lake, extracting primarily soda ash (used in glass-making and detergents) and borax. The company town of Trona, located next to the main plant, is home to the families of the 750 people who work at IMC.

SEARLES DRY LAKE, WITH THE TOWN OF TRONA VISIBLE IN THE UPPER LEFT

A REMOTE INDUSTRIAL SITE employing five hundred people on the shores of the Great Salt Lake makes most of the magnesium chloride produced in America, using minerals extracted from the lake's salty water. Forty thousand acres of evaporation ponds managed by the company use the dry air and sun's energy to concentrate the lake water into a brine that is then pumped into the lakeside plant. Inside the facility, an electrochemical process creates ingots of pure magnesium chloride. Magnesium chloride is one of those versatile "in-between" industrial chemicals, like borax. It's used, for example, in steel production, as a fire retardant in wood, as a dust-inhibitor for dirt roads, as a lubricant for wool, and as a supplement in cattle feed. For many years, according to the EPA, the plant was the nation's worst air polluter, releasing hundreds of tons of chlorine from its stacks each year, the majority of total chlorine gas emitted into the air nationwide. The agency eventually sought more than one hundred million dollars in fines, forcing the company that owned the plant at the time, the Magnesium Corporation of America, into bankruptcy. The plant is now owned by the American Magnesium Corporation.

AMERICAN MAGNESIUM CORPORATION

THE GREAT SALT LAKE, not surprisingly, is a major source of salt, but little of it is of the table salt variety. The Great Salt Lake Minerals Corporation is one of the largest saltworks on the lake. It manages two major sites with evaporation ponds: a nineteen-thousand-acre site at Little Mountain, where its plant is located, and a seventeen-thousand-acre field of ponds twenty-one miles across the lake, near Lakeside. The brine from the Lakeside field flows in an open canal underneath the lake surface (the concentrated brine is heavier than the water above it and stays in the canal). The brine takes as long as ten days to make the journey through the canal to the plant. Some 375 people work at two facilities here, extracting potassium sulfate (for fertilizers), sodium chloride (for industrial salt applications), sodium sulfate (for laundry detergent and glass), and magnesium chloride.

GREAT SALT LAKE MINERALS CORPORATION

SILVER PEAK LITHIUM PONDS
AND CONCENTRATORS

AT THE DUSTY MINING TOWN OF SILVER PEAK, in the remote Clayton Valley of western Nevada, a mining operation extracts lithium from the dry lake at the bottom of the valley. Lithium, well known for its pharmaceutical uses in treating conditions like bipolar disorders, is also used in the production of metals, ceramics, greases, batteries, and thermonuclear bombs. The operation, one of the world's largest producers of lithium hydroxide, started with the opening of a lithium carbonate brine plant in the 1960s. It is now owned by the Chemetall Corporation, based in Frankfurt, Germany.

OPEN-PIT MINES

In the flatlands of the lake beds, the most valuable minerals are unrecoverable, mixed too thoroughly, diluted to imperceptibility. In the mountains of the Great Basin, the easily mined, concentrated deposits of gold and silver were extracted in a great hurry in the late 1800s and early 1900s, leaving old mining towns like Virginia City, Tonopah, and Goldfield. Open-pit mining technology, pioneered in the Great Basin, enabled poor deposits to be viable if enough rock could be moved and processed by conveyors, trucks, trains, and slurry pipelines. With these technologies of mountain moving, the Great Basin has become the precious-metal mining center of America, extracting more gold and silver than any single state.

BINGHAM PIT

THE BASIN now has about fifty major open-pit mines, including some of the largest on earth, like the Bingham Pit. This active mine is the largest man-made hole in the country. Digging started in 1904, and the pit is now half a mile deep and more than two miles wide. It is expected to be enlarged continuously. It is owned and operated by Kennecott Utah Copper, a subsidiary of an international mining company, which employs twenty-four hundred people at the site and the nearby smelter.

ORE FROM THE BINGHAM PIT travels by conveyor from a crusher in the pit to a concentration plant a few miles away. A slurry pipeline then carries it several more miles to a smelter on the shore of the Great Salt Lake. Recently upgraded at a cost of nearly one billion dollars, the smelter features the nation's tallest smokestack; at 1,207 feet, it's just 35 feet shorter than the Empire State Building.

KENNECOTT SMELTER

THE LIBERTY PIT used to be the largest open pit in Nevada and was connected to Kennecott Nevada's large smelter in McGill, twenty miles away, by rail. The smelter was mostly torn down, and its stack imploded, in the 1980s. Much of the mining has stopped, but today ore is still extracted from the pit. It's concentrated to around 75 percent copper on site before being shipped by rail to a smelter in Arizona, and to China, via the port of Vancouver.

OVERLOOK AT THE LIBERTY PIT, NEAR RUTH, NEVADA

A NETWORK OF OPEN PITS around Mountain Pass, California, next to Interstate 15 on the way to Las Vegas, is the only domestic producer of "rare earths," a group of minerals used in a wide variety of industries. Samarium, for example, is used in the magnets in motors and speakers, including headphone electromagnets, while cerium oxide is used in television screens. Other rare earths are used in gasoline, fluorescent lighting, and medical equipment. The open-pit mines are operated by Molycorp, which is owned by Unocal.

THE MOUNTAIN PASS RARE-EARTH MINE

TAILINGS PILE AT THE RAND MINES

THE THREE MINES IN THIS COMPLEX at the top of the Mojave Desert—the Yellow Aster, Lamont, and Baltic—are collectively referred to as the Rand mines. They are located in a district littered with mineshafts and mining ruins from more than one hundred years of activity in the Red Mountain, Johannesburg, Randsburg region. The Rand mines are operated by the Glamis Gold Company, which also operates two other gold mines in Southern California. The Rand mines produce about eighty thousand ounces of gold annually (worth around thirty-four million dollars). The inhabited and scenic "ghost town" of Randsburg is in the center of this mining district.

US BORAX MINE

THE US BORAX MINE at Boron, in the Mojave, is the largest open-pit mine in California and the largest borate mine in the world, supplying more than half of the world's borates. The mine and refinery complex was established in the late 1920s, after a large source of borax was discovered here. Previously, borax was mined in Death Valley and hauled to the railway at Mojave by the famous "twenty-mule team." This mine consists of a pit measuring five hundred feet deep, more than a mile long, and half a mile wide. The substances obtained from the borates extracted here are used in numerous products, from soaps to jet fuels. Boron, for example, is an element with many applications in aerospace and military technologies, often as a component in high-strength fiber composites and in rocket fuels.

ROUND MOUNTAIN is one of a few dozen large gold-mining operations in Nevada, the state that produces about 75 percent of the gold mined in the United States. This open-pit mine is located seventy miles north of Tonopah in a long, wide valley. It has been in operation for a hundred years, though it only went into major production after World War II. The pit is about a mile and a half wide and a thousand feet deep and is surrounded by vast tailings and overburden piles removed from the pit. On an average day, the mine extracts approximately 250,000 tons of rock, from which 125 pounds of pure gold are made. At current values, the mine produces about one million dollars' worth of gold per day.

*RECTILINEAR WASTE ROCK HILLS
AT ROUND MOUNTAIN MINE*

TRAVERSING THE BASIN

The Great Basin is much taller than it is wide, extending from Mexico to central Oregon, and has always been something of a hurdle for cross-country travelers. Early settlers dreaded its dry, hot terrain (a legacy reflected in demonic place names like Devil's Hole and Death Valley). The infamous Donner-Reed party bogged down in the mud flats of the Great Salt Lake Desert, reaching the Sierra Nevada Mountains so late in the season that their journey to California took a famously macabre turn. Ironically, the area where they had the worst trouble is now famous as the site of numerous land speed records. The emptiness of the basin made it the final link in the nation's rail, road, and telephone networks, the place where east joins west. It is the middle of nowhere, on the way to everywhere else.

NO PLACE SUMS UP this notion better than the Bonneville Salt Flats. This large, flat expanse of white is a place people come to from great distances, to travel nowhere very quickly. Numerous land speed records have been achieved at Bonneville, on the vast and even natural pavement of salt: the land speed barriers of 300, 400, 500, and 600 miles per hour were all broken here over the years. The flats are a kind of tabula rasa, a blank slate of ground where people can experience a sense of nothingness. They also present the terrestrial version of a white gallery wall, making anything that is placed on it look good. And so it is a favored location for commercial photographers and television advertisers. The lens of hard white salt that floats on top of the thick muds of the Great Salt Lake Desert spends much of the year under water and is slowly disappearing. The hard-packed

area that is used for the races has shrunk from fifteen miles in length in 1950 to ten miles today, and the quality of the surface has decreased. A project to restore the hard-packed salt has been initiated by the chemical company that mines the flats and by the Bureau of Land Management, which owns the land.

BONNEVILLE SALT FLATS

THE GOLDEN SPIKE historic site, near the northeastern shore of the Great Salt Lake, is the point where the eastbound and westbound tracks for the first trans-continental railroad met. A visitors' center has been built here by the National Park Service. Initially, Union Pacific, which built the westbound track from Omaha, and Central Pacific, which built the eastbound track from California, refused to let their tracks meet, each wanting to have more of the territory under their jurisdiction. As a result, more than two hundred miles of par-allel grading was completed before Congress intervened and set the meeting point at Promontory Summit. On May 10, 1869, the tracks met and four golden spikes were ceremonially driven into the last tie laid. (The golden spikes were quickly removed for safe-keeping, though one has been missing ever since.)

THE MONUMENT AT THE GOLDEN SPIKE NATIONAL HISTORIC SITE HAS BEEN MOVED CLOSER TO THE VISITORS' CENTER TO PROTECT IT FROM VANDALISM.

FROM THE TIME OF THE DONNER-REED party through the opening of the Lincoln Highway (the nation's first continuous east-west road), the southern edge of the salt flats of western Utah has been an important historic means of continental convey-ance. Today the principal overland route through the area is Interstate 80, America's Main Street. It connects the George Washington Bridge in New York to the Bay Bridge in San Francisco. The longest stretch of highway without an exit (thirty-seven miles) is located along the flats between Bonneville and Knolls. The lack of visual stimulation is so severe that drivers are prone to dozing off and veering into the salt flats.

INTERSTATE 80, NEAR THE EDGE OF THE SALT FLATS

FEDERALAND:

THE COUNTRY'S COMMUNICATIONS infrastructure con-
verges into narrow service corridors that span the Great Basin,
connecting the population centers on the East and West Coasts.
A critical and singular microwave relay link, in the Great Salt
Lake Desert of Utah, was the site of an attack in 1960, in which
three consecutive towers, approximately forty miles apart, were
destroyed by time bombs. The military, along with AT&T and
IBM, spent a week restoring the connection. The perpetrators
were eventually arrested, convicted, served their time, and
were released.

WENDOVER PEAK, TOPPED
BY A MICROWAVE RELAY TOWER

THE RAIL LINE CELEBRATED by the Golden Spike, which runs around the northern end of the lake, was in use for thirty-five years before the Southern Pacific Railroad built a shortcut to bypass the steep grades and curves on the portion of the transcontinental railway between Ogden and Lucin. Called the Lucin Cutoff, it featured an engineering wonder of its time, a wooden trestle spanning the entire Great Salt Lake. Finished in 1904, the trestle rested on more than twenty-eight thousand piles, each about 120 feet long. In 1959, the wooden trestle was filled in with gravel, dividing the circulation of the lake into two halves—essentially forming two separate lakes. The northern part, with less drainage into it, has become saltier, while the southern part has become less salty. The 11.8-mile main span of the causeway across the lake remains one of the longest railway viaducts in the world.

*THE WATER NORTH OF THE CAUSEWAY
IS REDDER THAN THE WATER ON THE SOUTH
SIDE DUE TO HIGHER SALINITY AND A
BACTERIAL GROWTH WITH A RED TINGE.*

COMMUNITIES

Of course, many people do call the Great Basin home. Most live along the Wasatch Front, as the extended sprawl of the Salt Lake City region is known. Other population centers include Reno and its extending suburbs and the portion of the Las Vegas Valley that falls within the basin. Beyond these three nodes on the edges of the basin is a collection of hundreds of small communities that, in isolation, have evolved into some of the most curious places in the country.

GOLDFIELD, NEVADA

GOLDFIELD, NEVADA, stands apart from the many old mining towns in the basin, suspended in a state of partial disappearance. Goldfield was once the largest city in the state, with almost twenty thousand residents during the height of the gold-mining boom. Though it still has a couple hundred inhabitants and serves as the county seat for Esmeralda County, its downtown street grid, which once had curbstones and sidewalks, is lined with collapsed ruins and flattened piles of rubble. Some of the ruins are lived in or converted ingeniously into new types of dwellings, with the help of trailers, rocks, and debris. The surrounding landscape

is a churned-up mining area, littered with tailings piles and remnants of equipment and structures, underlain by hundreds of miles of tunnels and adits. Some of the stately turn-of-the-century buildings remain, decayed, abandoned, or in a partially restored state. The Goldfield Hotel, the largest remaining structure in town, was once one of the great hotels of the West. Over the past couple of decades, millions of dollars have been spent in failed attempts to restore the hotel. (At one point, rooms had even been booked, years in advance, by a Japanese tour group.) But even the modern improvements are now decaying.

*THE ROAD TO THE MAIN SETTLEMENT
IN THE SKULL VALLEY IS POSTED.*

IN THE MIDDLE OF UTAH'S REMOTE SKULL VALLEY, a band

of Goshute Indians lives on a reservation too dry for farming and too remote for a casino. The reservation is home to approximately sixty Native Americans, who reside in a dozen or so households. Yet they wield tremendous power. The reservation is in the middle of one of the highest concentrations of hazardous land uses, between Dugway Proving Ground and the West Desert Hazardous Industries Area. Plumes of chlorine rise from the magnesium plant at the north end of the valley, while the Intermountain Power Plant (a massive coal-fired electrical plant built in the middle of Utah by the Los Angeles Department of Water and Power) operates to the south. The band's leader, claiming that his land is not much good for anything else, has contracted with a company representing several eastern utility companies to work on building a radioactive waste repository on their land. Because the Goshute are a sovereign nation, the state of Utah, which opposes the idea, may or may not be able to stop it, and the plan looks more likely if things go poorly at Yucca Mountain. Money has already started flowing to the band from the deal, and construction on the reservation is increasing along with the population.

THE ONLY OTHER SETTLEMENT IN SKULL VALLEY

is the abandoned town of Iosepa, once a community of more than two hundred Polynesians who settled here in 1889 to be closer to the center of the Mormon Church. A few years later, leprosy broke out in the community, leading to the formation of Utah's only known leper colony (though it consisted of just a few people). By 1917, the last members of the community returned to Hawaii. Almost all of the structures are now gone, though several foundations at the old townsite are visible. A cemetery near the townsite contains the graves of many of the settlers as well as a large stone monument to the community.

*GRAVEYARD WITH POLYNESIAN
MONUMENT IN UTAH'S SKULL VALLEY*

ONCE A YEAR, one of the largest and most transgressive temporary communities in the nation forms in the middle of one of the emptiest places in America: the Black Rock Desert in northwestern Nevada, the country's largest, flattest stretch of ground. The notorious annual Burning Man festival is an unsurpassed public bacchanal, drawing about thirty thousand people. Features include rave areas, theme tent complexes, art cars, swings, performance stages, and arty happenings. The weeklong festival culminates with a ritualistic procession and the igniting of a forty-foot-tall humanoid effigy adorned with fluorescent tubes.

THE TEMPORARY CITY
OF BURNING MAN

ANOTHER INTERMITTENT FREE COMMUNITY in the Great Basin is located in the Imperial Valley near the Salton Sea. Slab City is an assemblage of mostly recreational vehicles; a community that formed on its own, without any apparent organizational force. Located at the site of a former military base on the edge of the Chocolate Mountains, an active bombing range, Slab City gets its name from the prevalence of concrete aprons—or slabs—at the site. A network of roadways and slabs accommodates a community of up to a few thousand occupants in the cooler winter months. The populace is comprised of all sorts, from road warriors living in buses that haven't moved in twenty years to snowbirds—retired folks who migrate to warmer climes in their recreational vehicles each winter. This eclectic mix of people gets along well, and residents seem to enjoy the variety of attitudes at Slab City.

SLAB CITY VIEWED FROM THE AIR

CHRIST
OF THE
ANDES

A GREAT EXAMPLE of inspired individual creativity is Cathedral Canyon, a small natural canyon that has been transformed into a rambling grotto of icons, statues, and text panels. Religious in overall tone, the site has many secular elements as well. Though untended, it's open to the public and meant to be stumbled upon. It is best viewed at night, when the multicolored lighting system illuminates the individual displays, which are laid out along the main pathway and tucked into walls and bushes in the canyon. Cathedral Canyon was built mostly by Roland Wiley, a lawyer from Las Vegas, who bought the 15,800-acre Hidden

LANDMARKS
OF INDIVIDUALITY

In the Great Basin, the landscape dominates, and romantic notions about space and isolation flourish. Visionaries are pulled into this space for some of the same reasons that draw radioactive waste into the basin: it is often the path of least resistance. Given space, creative drives to respond to this landscape can blossom into landmarks that express qualities of the place as much as they reflect the characters who made them. Unique individual interactions with the land reveal new ways of seeing and new views of the thing seen.

THE SUSPENSION BRIDGE, STAIRWAY, AND MONUMENTS OF CATHEDRAL CANYON

Hills Ranch, on which the canyon lies, in 1972. Wiley worked on the canyon over the next thirty years, mainly on weekend trips from Las Vegas, until his death in 1993. Vandalism has recently taken its toll on the remote site.

THUNDER MOUNTAIN

NEAR THE TOWN OF IMLAY, in northern Nevada, is a unique site that stands as monument to the tragic plight of Native Americans. Called Thunder Mountain, it is a complex of sculptures and handmade structures created from debris found in the area (car parts, bottles, wheels, railroad ties, etc.) and held together in a matrix of concrete. Most of it was erected between 1967 and 1975 by a man named Rolling Mountain Thunder, who lived here for many years. The complex consists of a two-story structure (a second large building, known as the hostel, burned down in the late 1980s), surrounded by pathways and sculptures. Rolling Mountain Thunder, who was born Frank Van Zandt in 1911, committed suicide in 1989.

*ONE OF THE NUMEROUS
FEATURES ALONG GURU ROAD*

GURU ROAD, in northern Nevada, is another unusual, unten-ded site. It is a quarter-mile-long dirt road that is lined with sculptures and stones inscribed with the quips and witticisms of its maker, Duane Williams, also known as "Doobie" and "the Guru." Features include the Desert Broadcast Imagination Station, a hut fashioned as a sort of television control center with TV frames as windows. The road, located outside of the remote desert town of Gerlach, on the edge of the Black Rock Desert, was built over several years before the Guru died in 1995.

THE TREE OF UTAH is an artwork constructed between 1982 and 1986 by the Swedish artist Karl Momen. Born in Iran, Momen painted portraits of Stalin and the Shah of Iran early in his career, then studied architecture in Stuttgart, Germany, where he was influenced by Russian Constructivism and Surrealism. It has been said that the vastness and relative emptiness of the Bonneville Salt Flats moved him to create the eighty-seven-foot-tall tree. The sculpture's six spheres are coated with natural rock and minerals found within the state of Utah, and the pods below symbolize the changing of the seasons, when trees naturally transform themselves. The cost of building the tree, reportedly more than one million dollars, was covered entirely by Momen. The tree now belongs to the state of Utah.

TREE OF UTAH

SOME OF THE CONTEMPORARY ART AT THE GOLDWELL OPEN AIR MUSEUM AT RHYOLITE

RHYOLITE, situated in the Bullfrog gold-mining district in southern Nevada, is a picturesque ghost town that has developed a split identity as a contemporary sculpture park. A number of multistory facades still stand from the town's heyday, around 1910, when the population was near ten thousand. (The ruined bank building is well known from an Ansel Adams photograph.) A well-preserved bottle house (a house for which bottles—items that were in abundance in booming mining towns—were the principal building material) is watched over by volunteers and the Bureau of Land Management. Another structure, the old railway station, has been lived in until recently. The collection of large sculptures started to appear in the 1980s when a Belgian artist named Albert Szukalski began making fiberglass casts of area residents. He erected a life-size sculptural Last Supper, populated with ghostly fiberglass forms. Works by other sculptors followed over the years, including a massive pink nude constructed out of cinder blocks. The park changed hands after Szukalski's death in 2000 and is now operated as the Goldwell Open Air Museum.

HUNDREDS OF TALL DATE PALM TREES form unusual patterns at the remote interstate town of Desert Center, California. The project was started years ago by the owner of the town, Stanley Ragsdale, who trucked the trees from a date farm near Indio, fifty miles away. Many of the seventy-foot-tall trees, which were originally grown by King Gillette, the inventor of the safety razor, are now dying due to irrigation problems. Ragsdale has died as well.

DESERT CENTER

SALVATION MOUNTAIN, just south of the Salton Sea, is a hillside that has been painted and formed into a monumental sculpture, a terraced escarpment with religious messages, as well as a vaulted structure of mud and hay, held up by a network of tree limbs. It was created by Leonard Knight over the past fifteen years using donated paint and adobe made on site.

SALVATION MOUNTAIN

SUN TUNNELS is an artwork by Nancy Holt on a barren plain beyond the western side of the Great Salt Lake. Completed in 1976, it consists of four large concrete tubes laid out in an open X configuration. The "tunnels," measuring nine feet in diameter and eighteen feet long, are pierced by holes that vary in size and correspond with the pattern of selected celestial constellations, including Draco, Perseus, Columbia, and Capricorn. The X is arranged so that the tunnels line up with the sun at the summer and winter solstices.

SUN TUNNELS

SPIRAL JETTY

ACROSS THE LAKE is *Spiral Jetty*, made by Holt's husband, Robert Smithson. A basalt spiral measuring fifteen hundred feet long and fifteen feet wide, the jetty protrudes from the shore of the Great Salt Lake on submerged land leased from the government. For most of its life *Spiral Jetty* has been invisible, lying a few feet under the fluctuating surface level of the lake. Smithson built the piece with the help of a local contractor over a period of fifteen days in 1970, at a time when the water was low (4,195 feet above sea level). The Dia Foundation in New York acquired the piece from Smithson's estate in 1999. It subsequently reemerged, concurrent with a major retrospective of Smithson's work.

MICHAEL HEIZER has been building the largest modern sculpture in the world in a remote valley in the Great Basin for thirty years. His *Complex City* in the Nevada desert consists of a number of building-size structures made of mounded earth, gravel, and concrete. The series of complexes surrounds a central "court" that, when finished, may be as much as a mile long. Located fifty miles from the nearest community, the site is off the phone and electrical grids and is one of only a few structures in a vast valley. Heizer has lived and worked here for much of his life.

THE GATE TO COMPLEX CITY, *WHICH IS CLOSED TO THE PUBLIC*

ONE OF THE MOST COMMITTED VISIONARIES of the Great Basin is Marta Beckett, a classically trained ballerina from New York who, the legend goes, came to the isolated town of Death Valley Junction in 1968 to have a flat tire repaired and essentially never left. After falling in love with the abandoned community hall of the colonnaded town center, she developed it into the Amargosa Opera House. Beckett began performing there regularly, sometimes with only her painted murals—portraying an audience of sixteenth-century Spanish royalty, clerics, gypsies, and revelers—in attendance. Now in her eighties and still at it, she is the embodiment of the romantic desert visionary whom others can only imagine.

AMARGOSA OPERA HOUSE

CLUI WENDOVER

The Center for Land Use Interpretation has established an interpretive district in the heart of Federaland, in the middle of the edge. From this point, at Wendover, Utah, the Center offers public programs, displays, and tours of the region.

Wendover is located where the basin and range of Nevada spill into the flats of the Great Salt Lake Desert, where the ranching and mining of northeastern Nevada merge with the proving grounds and practice ranges of northwestern Utah. It is a community split by one of the most culturally abrupt state lines in the nation, as it divides the conservative Mormon state of Utah, where even coffee drinking is frowned upon, from the twenty-four-hour liquor, gambling, and legal prostitution that are available in Nevada. The Utah side is a cluster of trailers, based on an old railway town, and is dominated by the remains of an airfield. West Wendover (on the Nevada side) has five casinos, which employ 80 percent of the local population. The town's official motto is "On the Edge."

THE CENTER'S WENDOVER FACILITIES INCLUDE BUILDINGS NEXT TO THE WENDOVER BOMBING RANGE.

THE CENTER'S FACILITIES are on the Utah side, on the edge of town, amid the ruins and relics of a mostly abandoned and torn-down military base. Wendover Air Base was the largest bomber-training base during World War II, with more than six hundred buildings, three million acres of bombing range, and

twenty thousand people at its peak. Toward the end of the war, the crews of the *Enola Gay* and *Bock's Car* moved in for six months and began testing and training for atomic bomb missions, even before any nuclear device was tested. Led by Col. Paul Tibbets, the crew helped to test different delivery mechanisms by dropping dummy bombs and prototypes into the Wendover salt flats and the Salton Sea, at the southern end of the Great Basin, with scientists heading back and forth to Los Alamos with new designs. Dozens of these dummy bombs no doubt remain buried in the still-restricted Wendover Range and at the bottom of the sea.

The Center's exhibit halls and self-guided tour materials describe the immediate area as well as the broader region of the Great Basin. On the local, microcosmic scale, they discuss the recent history of the airfield, from World War II to the present, showing how many of the buildings have been repurposed. Col. Tibbets's office, for example, is now a self-storage facility, and the hangar that once housed the *Enola Gay* has been used for Tesla-like high-voltage experiments, as a location for the 2003 film *Hulk*, and as a backdrop for REO Speedwagon concerts.

Some exhibits serve as a kind of scavenger hunt, guiding people, in a limited way, around the points of interest in the area. On the macrocosmic level, the Center's displays provide a broad view about the way land is used in this perceived void.

A RADIO TOWER BUILT BY THE ARTIST DEBORAH STRATMAN ENABLES VISITORS TO LISTEN TO THE INFRASTRUCTURAL FREQUENCIES OF THE REGION.

Also on display is the work of individuals and groups that come to Wendover under the auspices of the Center's Wendover Residence Program, which brings creative people from all over the nation and the world to live in, investigate, and interpret this unique and compelling environment.

*THE OFF-THE-GRID WORKSPACE
CONSTRUCTED BY THE DESIGN/BUILD
COLLECTIVE SIMPARCH AT THE EDGE
OF THE SALT FLATS*

The Center for Land Use Interpretation has established these programs in Wendover to serve both as a destination and as a point of departure. People can find their way to the site and help themselves to information about the region and exhibits located around the area. Then they can venture back out into the landscape, to explore and discover on their own.

ACKNOWLEDGMENTS

The Center for Land Use Interpretation is composed of a dedicated group of staff and volunteers, including Michael Asbill, Steve Badgett, Lisa Boulanger, Deena Capparelli, Julia Christensen, Matthew Coolidge, Mark Curtin, Sean Dockray, Corinna Fish, John Fitchen, Heather Frazar, Jennifer Gabrys, Oswaldo Gonzales, Dara Greenwald, Cindy Hooper, Chris Kahle, Michael Kassner, Erik Knutzen, Mathias Kolehmainen, Zelig Kurland, Carrie Lincourt, Ben Loescher, Angela Loughry, Suzanna Mast, Ryan McKinley, Josh McPhee, Lize Mogel, Richard Pell, John Reed, Caitlin Rocklen, Steve Rowell, Elon Schoenholz, Bianca Siegl, Sarah Simons, Melinda Stone, Dave Vamos, Igor Vamos, Kazys Varnelis, and Fiona Whitton.

We would like to thank the following exhibition, production, and educational institutions, which have assisted us through our first ten years of existence: Art Center College of Design; Atlanta College of Art; Aurora Picture Show; Beall Center for Art and Technology; California College of the Arts; California Institute for the Arts; Columbia University Graduate School of Architecture, Planning and Preservation; Contemporary Arts Center Cincinatti; De Verbeelding; DiverseWorks Art Space; Fort Asperen Foundation; Headlands Center for the Arts; Institute for Advanced Architecture; Institute For Figuring; Karl Ernst Osthaus-Museum; Los Angeles Contemporary Exhibitions; MIT List Center for Visual Arts; Museum of Contemporary Art, Los Angeles; The Museum of Jurassic Technology; Neuer Aachen Kunstverein; Otis College of Art and Design; Princeton School of Architecture; Pomona College Museum of Art; Royal College of Art; Sonoma County Museum; Storefront for Art and Architecture; University Art Museum Santa Barbara; University of California, Los Angeles; University of Utah; Whitney Museum of Art; Witte de With Center for Contemporary Art; and Yerba Buena Center for the Arts.

We are especially grateful to the following organizations, which make the Center's programming possible: The Annenberg Foundation, Creative Capital, The Nathan Cummings Foundation, The Danielson Foundation, The Durfee Foundation, Getty Grant Program, John Simon Guggenheim Memorial Foundation, The Gunk Foundation, The Hemingway Western Studies Center, Lannan Foundation, LEF Foundation, The Los Angeles County Arts Commission, Los Angeles Cultural Affairs Department, The National Endowment for the Arts, National Video Resources, The Nevada Humanities Committee, The Peter Norton Family Foundation, The David and Lucille Packard Foundation, The Pioneer Documentary Fund, The Puffin Foundation, and The Andy Warhol Foundation for the Visual Arts.